PRAISE FOR DR. BOEHM & *IS YOUR LIFE SUCCESSFUL?*

"Dr. Frank Boehm, an astute lifelong observer of human nature as a beloved and respected physician, artfully weaves the wisdom he gleaned from conversations with 200 remarkable people into a thought provoking and compassionate guide for fulfillment and success."

–Bill Frist, U.S. Senator

"We all want to be happy and successful. Frank has put his magic touch on a book filled with his inspiration and wisdom and with insight from people of every walk of life. This is a book you will want to read more than once."

–Crystal Gayle,
Grammy Award-Winning Singer/Songwriter

"What a fun guide to our own lives, and for people of all ages! Everyone needs this book because everyone wants to be successful, and the best way to do that is to learn from others. Frank Boehm found 200 such role models for us. We identify with them because Frank listened so carefully and tenderly to their stories…just like the superb physician that he is. Frank shows us the reset button in our lives so that we can become our best selves."

–Jim Cooper, U.S. Congressman

"This book is filled with heart, humor, and amazing wake-up calls–as inspiring and original as it is fun. You might even expand your personal definition of a successful life like I did."

–Arnold Shapiro,
Academy Award & Emmy Award-Winning Producer

"As we age, our perspective on what success is matures, as Frank demonstrates with his many interviews in Is Your Life Successful. We can benefit from these insights to think about our own lives and take steps to ensure that the success we pursue is in the final analysis, that which we ourselves truly value."

—Senator Bob Corker

"Frank has been my friend always and has given me the best advice throughout the years. There's no doubt, he's one of the best at what he does. Many people go to their grave never realizing their accomplishments or their self-worth and I'm sure some do, thinking they were more successful than they really were! This book will shed light on what success feels like to people from different walks of life and will leave you pondering and asking yourself if you feel like your life's been successful. You may be surprised by your answer!"

—Tanya Tucker,
Award-winning Singer and Songwriter

"Dr. Boehm's gifts as a physician and scholar are surpassed only by his extraordinary talent for illuminating the metacognitive perspective on human experience. His earlier writings, from *Doctors Cry, Too* to decades of editorials published in *The Tennessean* and other media, have given readers a special sensitivity to the emotional and cognitive manifestations of healing, living, and dying. Here, Dr. Boehm poignantly explores the ages and stages of meaning-making through people sharing their own compelling stories, giving us all food for thought as we reflect on our own."

—Jeff Balser, MD, PhD. CEO,
Vanderbilt University Medical Center

IS YOUR LIFE SUCCESSFUL?

IS YOUR
LIFE
SUCCESSFUL?

ANSWERS AND ANECDOTES FROM
OVER 200 EVERYDAY PEOPLE

FRANK H. BOEHM, MD

TURNER
PUBLISHING COMPANY

Turner Publishing Company
Nashville, Tennessee
www.turnerpublishing.com

Is Your Life Successful? Answers and Anecdotes from Over 200 Everyday People

Cover design: Grace Cavalier
Book design: Mallory Collins

Names: Boehm, Frank H., author.
Title: Is your life successful? : answers and anecdotes from over 200
    everyday people / by Frank H. Boehm MD.
Description: 1st Edition. | Nashville, Tennessee : Turner Publishing
    Company, 2022. | Includes bibliographical references and index. |

Identifiers: LCCN 2021021836 | ISBN 9781684426973 (paperback) | ISBN
    9781684426980 (hardback) | ISBN 9781684426997 (ebook)
Subjects: LCSH: Success. | Quality of life.
Classification: LCC BF637.S8 B574 2022 | DDC 158.1--dc23
LC record available at https://lccn.loc.gov/2021021836

Printed in the United States of America

*Dedicated to Julie, who has
made my life successful*

CONTENTS

FOREWORD

AMONG ANCIENT AND RECORDED TRADITIONS, perhaps none is more meaningful or more enduring than what is referred to as the Wisdom Writings of a people. Jewish Wisdom Writings represent one of the greatest examples of these collections, both in terms of the questions it hopes to raise and the answers it hopes to share with us. To that end, in the opening chapters of the Talmud (the Jewish collection of jurisprudence), the ancient rabbis, writing two thousand years ago, began that sacred text with simple questions and profound answers on how to build a successful existence during our time on this earth. In the Sayings of the Sages (the *Pirkei Avot*) they write: Who is wise? The one who learns something from everyone. Who is a hero? The one who can control both his anger and his passions. Who is to be honored? The one who can value the worth of everyone. And perhaps most importantly, Who is rich, or successful? The one who is content and at peace with his lot, with what one already possesses, in ways both large and small.

That tradition is shared, among others, with the author of this book of insight, Doctor Frank Boehm. In it, Dr. Boehm adds to the continuity of this unbroken chain of Wisdom literature, still attempting to meet the challenge of searching for kernels of wisdom and extracting them from a variety of human vessels, regardless of their station or status. Dr. Boehm believes that within every human soul, a still, small voice may offer a unique glimpse into the meaning and worth of living a purposeful life. Dr. Boehm has narrowed the lens to focus on the different meanings of success and what defies the often-elusive quest to define it. Here, in his book, he gives countless examples from people of various genders, ages, educational backgrounds, and life experiences, those who come from all walks of life. Each brings profound wisdom into our view; every single one of them has insight that can intrigue or inspire us, whether we choose to incorporate that knowledge into our lives or not.

That is ultimately our choice to make, of course: but through Dr. Boehm's interviews and subsequent compilation of those teachings of others, and of his own shared musings, he has given us a treasure trove of motivation to reflect upon our own lives and upon our own articulation of living a successful life by our words and examples. More importantly, he has offered us a sacred pathway to adapt and make changes and course corrections to our lives, no matter our age or stage along the journey. In that sense, Dr. Boehm has given his readers a work that is priceless beyond measure. In these uncertain times, it is a particularly valuable gift to us.

Rabbi Mark Schiftan
May 2020

INTRODUCTION

HOW WOULD YOU DEFINE A SUCCESSFUL LIFE? I
had just turned seventy-five, approaching the end of a long
career in medicine, when it occurred to me that I had never really
thought about this question. My initial answer was, of course
I was successful. I was a physician at Vanderbilt University
Medical Center, and I had raised three children who had good
careers and were all happily married and wonderful parents to
our nine grandchildren. I had a loving, incredibly happy marriage of over three decades and many close and loving friends.
What more was there? Still, after all the years and all I had experienced, I wondered, was my life truly a successful one?

The more I thought about it, the more I was intrigued by the
thought that there must be a wide spectrum to the definition of a
successful life. I began with Webster's definition of *successful*:
"accomplishing an aim or purpose, having achieved popularity,
profit, or distinction." This seemed a rather narrow and somewhat limited definition of *successful*. I believed that the answer
to my question was more layered than a few responses. I realized the answer would be dependent upon the many aspects and
measures of an individual's life and that the question to ask was
not only what a successful life is but also what has determined
or will determine whether someone feels they have achieved it.

I began by asking several individuals what they thought a successful life encompassed, and the responses I received were often initially generic and nonpersonal, similar to Webster's definition, ranging from monetary accumulation, fame, and societal stature to recognition in business, science, medicine, law, and sports, to name just a few. However, I was searching for an objective definition, one that I could use as a template on the subject and one that would be more encompassing for many individuals who may not have achieved huge financial gains, fame, or societal stature and recognition.

I began the search for my answer by asking people of different socioeconomic classes, professions, and ages their definition of a successful life. That question led me on a two-year journey that resulted in email responses from and interviews of over two hundred individuals and confirmed my belief that there were indeed many different aspects to the definition and a multitude of ways for one to conclude whether they had lived a successful life. Dr. Alan Graber, eighty-four years old, a colleague and retired physician, agreed: "The definition of a successful life lies within each of us and cannot be defined by others, by societal norms, by business or professional or athletic accomplishments, by financial measurements, even by a rag to riches story, or by righteousness. A successful life takes many forms. There are no universal metrics."

I believe that our individual definitions are unique to our experiences in life and our age, just as our DNA is a biological and specific signature for each of us. I concluded that a successful life would be one in which an individual believed that they had either maximized their genetic potential and

environmental influences or had been able to minimize or overcome negative aspects of their genetic inheritance and environmental influences. This relatively simple, objective, and generic
definition seemed to allow for an equalitarian approach to defining a successful life and would allow for many individuals to
feel as if their lives had indeed been successful by a definition
unlike Webster's.

Using this objective and generic definition of a successful
life, a child born to parents of low intelligence and raised in
an economically deprived environment and a crime-ridden
neighborhood may not reach a high level of intellectual or monetary success, yet may, nonetheless, graduate from high school and
perhaps a trade school, become gainfully employed, marry, have
children, and develop close friendships that allow for many happy
moments. These individuals, I believe, when asked whether they
have been successful, might answer that they have indeed lived a
successful life. They were able to minimize and overcome their
disadvantageous genetic potential and environmental influences.

Similarly, consider a child born to loving and nurturing college-
educated parents who had achieved a comfortable lifestyle
working in respected professions. If that child not only graduates from college but also becomes a lawyer working in a prestigious firm, one could say that this child had maximized their
favorable genetic potential and environmental influences and
therefore would consider their life to be successful. I sought to
confirm this objective definition.

As I began to interview many individuals, however, I realized that there were those in our society who had not been able

to meet this objective and generic definition but who nonetheless believed they had lived or were living successful lives. They had not been able to maximize their positive genetic potential and environmental influences, nor had they minimized the negative either. For these individuals and many others, a different set of defining characteristics would aid in their definition of a successful life. Most of the individuals from whom I obtained a definition did not answer the question based on my objective definition; almost all responded with subjective and personal aspects to their definition, such as being happy, loving work, and having a loving family and friends.

Is Your Life Successful? is a collection of definitions from over two hundred individuals from all walks of life that attempts to reveal foundational principles of what each considers to be the definition of a successful life. I received many definitions via email and just as many by direct interviews. I took extensive notes without tape-recording responses and placed the definitions on my computer shortly after the meetings. I also shared what I wrote with many of the participants.

I have included individuals who are young and old, poor and wealthy. I interviewed people of various faiths, the homeless, the working poor, the physically and intellectually challenged, the terminally ill, as well as individuals from a large variety of professions, including nurses, doctors, social workers, songwriters and musicians, real estate agents, security personnel, Uber drivers, civic volunteers, firefighters, reverends and rabbis, administrators, entrepreneurs, teachers, secretaries, and lawyers. I interviewed a professor of philosophy, professor of biochemistry, priest, police officer, restaurant owner, artist, public relations professional, hairdresser, speech therapist, accountant, veterinarian, comedian, music producer, psychiatrist, Emmy winner, and Oscar winner. I also sat down with famous entertainers, two former United States senators and a former and current United States congressman, and the CEO of the prestigious Vanderbilt University Medical Center.

While most individuals contributing to these definitions reside in Tennessee, individuals from multiple states including California, Colorado, New York, Kentucky, Georgia, Minnesota, Illinois, Indiana, and Florida also made contributions. In some cases, individuals, especially the younger ones, when expressing their definition(s), were only able to define success without being able to consider whether they had succeeded in achieving it. Their definition was something they hoped to accomplish someday. Those in the older categories were able to not only define success but also comment on whether they felt they had fulfilled their definition.

I decided to separate the definitions of success by the age of the respondent rather than by socioeconomic class. Individuals below the age of twenty-five I label the Young, and those twenty-five to forty-nine years of age I call the Maturing Age. Those individuals fifty to seventy-five years of age, I label the Mature, and I refer to the group of individuals over seventy-five years as the Older. I did this to highlight the fact that as we grow older, we become more experienced in what truly matters in life and are also better able to measure the elements of what constitutes a successful life. It has been said that good judgment comes from experience and experience comes from bad judgment. The longer we live the more we experience and the more we understand how to act and what it is we wish to attain. I was interested to evaluate if this premise is reasonable and accurate.

Within the pages of this book, I have delved more deeply into many individual lives in each of the age groups and how they view a successful life. I devote a chapter to my personal definition, both objective and subjective, and conclude with a chapter on observations of my findings and, along the way, provide my opinions on a variety of issues, including my philosophy of life, life after death, the importance of awareness, making a positive impact on the lives of others, love, friendship, happiness, and faith.

Through my research I found individual definitions to be objective, subjective, or both and discovered the overwhelming majority to be quite egalitarian and not based solely on financial status, fame, or societal status. I believe readers will find comfort in the simplicity of defining a successful life and that it need not be determined by money or fame but rather by the basic elements of life that create within each of us the feeling or state of being successful.

We define and measure so much in our lives but rarely attempt to define for ourselves a successful life or measure whether we have lived up to that definition. I believe it is important for all of us to consider what we believe would constitute a successful life and then to assess whether we have met that definition or are at least on the way to meeting that definition. Perhaps it is time for all of us to consider this task an important one to undertake.

CHAPTER 1

HOW DO WE DEFINE
A SUCCESSFUL LIFE?

"Success and achievement are not the same thing. Achievement is something you reach or attain, like a goal. Success, in contrast, is a feeling or a state of being." Simon Sinek

"Money can buy you many things, but it can't buy you an extra minute in the day." Bill Gates

"A meaningful life includes the struggle to become more morally fit." David Brooks

"A calm and modest life brings more happiness than the pursuit of success combined with constant restlessness." Albert Einstein

"Real success in life comes when we learn to build and sustain relationships, develop emotional intelligence, and then go out of our way to make somebody else's life better." Reverend Clay Stauffer

ALL OF US ARE BORN WITH GENETIC MATERIAL inherited from our parents. The DNA contained in each of our cells is a combination of our parents' DNA, and because of this, much of who we are and what we become is based on this fact of life, and as a result we have no choice but to accept what was given to us at birth. In his book *21 Lessons for the 21st Century*, Yuval Noah Harari goes as far as to write, "Morality, art, spirituality, and creativity are universal human abilities embedded in our DNA."[1] I would add that much of our personalities, desires, sexual orientation, interests, and people skills are also embedded in our DNA. In addition, so much of who we are and what we become is determined by the environment in which we are raised. This two-pronged effect on our lives is often referred to as nature and nurture.

It has been said that nature loads the gun and nurture pulls the trigger; however, there is more to this process of human development. Obviously, the nature part is out of our control, so from the very beginning of our lives, what is to become of us is somewhat predetermined. But there is also an inherent aspect of our lives that is clearly determined by our environment, will, and determination that goes beyond the obvious gifts of DNA. But this is not the entire story. While there are limits imposed by our genetic makeup and influences brought about by numerous environmental factors, we do possess the ability to fashion successful lives for ourselves.

The journey on the road to a successful life demands that one makes certain critical choices along the way that will result in a better chance of beating the odds of genetic potential and environmental influences. How those choices are made is based on many complex situations. A child who looks around and sees only poverty, deprivation, and abuse may make a conscious thought to create a different life and in so doing will look for opportunities to educate themselves or move away from negative influences. Other times, it may just be good luck that allows for one to maximize their chances for living a successful life.

In the movie *Sliding Doors*, the actress Gwyneth Paltrow wakes up one morning and leaves her sleeping boyfriend to take a train to work. Upon arriving at work, she is notified that her job has been eliminated and she has been terminated. Clearly upset, she rushes down the subway stairs to board the train back home. As she approaches the train's closing sliding door, she slips inside and takes a seat. The next scene in the movie shows her rushing down the stairs as she had in the previous scene, but this time she does *not* make it on time and the sliding door closes, leaving her to wait for the next train. From that moment, the scenes are split depicting how life unfolds when she makes it through the sliding door and when she does not. In the former scenario, Paltrow returns home unexpectedly early and finds her boyfriend in bed with another woman; in the latter, she returns home to find her boyfriend alone in bed, his lover having just left. The movie depicts how each of these two scenarios unfolds and drastically changes her life.

In so many ways, each time we choose one path over another,

we are invoking the foundational principle of this story of sliding doors. Turn left at the traffic light and we arrive safely at our destination. Take a right for a quicker route and we are involved in a crash that takes our life. Decide at the last moment to attend a party and wind up meeting the person who becomes your loving spouse for life. Most of the time we are unaware of how each of our choices plays such a monumental role in our lives, yet each often does, nonetheless.

Choices and luck are critical elements of how our lives unfold despite the enormous influences of nature and nurture. There are, of course, many individuals whose genetic gifts have resulted in a high level of intelligence or talent, and many use these gifts as a springboard to a successful career and life. Unfortunately, the mere gift of intelligence or talent does not guarantee a successful life. Often individuals with a very high level of intelligence are unable to develop social skills that are often needed for advancement at school and work as well as for being able to obtain close and nurturing relationships. There are many stories of gifted humans who fall into the abyss of drugs and alcohol addiction and many other negative situations in life.

The same can be said of those whose environment and nurturing are excellent. The neighborhood they lived in was peaceful and tranquil. The friendships that were developed at school were well-balanced and accepting, and each day at work or play was devoid of stress. Parents were supportive and helpful, and there were no economic stresses or hunger in their lives. Yet, even in these healthy environmental situations, a successful life may not be achieved. So much of who we are and what we are to become is dependent on an inner drive that makes us aware of a need to do better, go further, study and work harder, understand more, and reach for a purposeful life. This is the part of life in which our DNA and the environment we grew up in does not influence us. It may limit to some degree what we will become, but it cannot and does not define us in a comprehensive manner. Sandra Day O'Connor, the first woman to become a Supreme Court justice, once spoke on this very issue to an interviewer, describing "an indefinable signal within me which has told me each time when I'm faced with a tough choice, which way to go." And as a note she wrote herself stated, "Don't let fate take over. You can influence your destiny."[2]

There are also many individuals who are born to parents without high intelligence or without a nurturing environment yet are noted to be of exceptional intelligence and who eventually become extremely successful. The nature and nurture aspects of our lives will not necessarily aid nor inhibit us from eventually defining our lives as successful regardless of yearly income or recognition of significant accomplishments. We are more than our DNA and environment.

In his book *Start with Why*, author Simon Sinek describes how a group of high-performing entrepreneurs gather yearly at MIT near Boston to listen to speakers and to discuss among themselves and others issues related to a variety of subjects.[3] Sinek, who was invited as a guest speaker several years ago, tells of another speaker who asked the group of forty to fifty business owners how many had achieved their financial goals, and approximately 80 percent raised their hands. Sinek then notes that the follow-up question of how many felt successful resulted in an answer that surprised him: 80 percent of the raised hands went down.

Sinek explains, "Here was a room full of some of America's brightest entrepreneurs, many of them multimillionaires, some of whom don't need to work anymore if they don't want to, yet most of them still didn't feel as if they had succeeded. In fact, many of them reported that they'd lost something since they started their businesses. They reminisced about the days when they didn't have any money and were working out of their basements, trying to get things going. They longed for the feeling they used to have." Sinek concludes that these financially successful entrepreneurs knew what they did, and they knew how they did it. But for many, they no longer knew why. This phenomenon has been described before. Many have opined that it is the trip that brings the most thrills and joy, but reaching the destination often yields a feeling of letdown.

I remember how much I enjoyed writing my first book, *Doctors Cry, Too*, but also how much that joy was mitigated when the book was completed. It was the process of writing that brought me pleasure and a feeling of success. So it was, it seems, with the successful businessmen who raised their hands with the first question but not the next that asked if they felt successful. Making money and being successful in business did not create a feeling of success.

I am not surprised research has shown that a successful life is so much more than being successful in business and making a great deal of money. Money can make life easier and livable, but at a certain level it can no longer buy happiness or a feeling of being successful. Sinek points this out when he writes, "Success and achievement are not the same thing. Achievement is something you reach or attain, like a goal. Success, in contrast, is a feeling or a state of being."[4]

As I began to put this book together, I thought I would separate those individuals from whom I had received definitions into the three major socioeconomic classes. It seemed reasonable to believe that those individuals in the upper class would have quite different definitions from those in the middle and lower class and would also have certain identifiable definitions based on their income and class. However, I found it difficult to objectively define the various socioeconomic classes.

Can we accurately use the income level or net worth of an individual to place them into upper, middle, and lower class, or are other aspects of life such as career or importance of their job a better criterion? Do college professors or other professionals belong in the middle class simply because they are not in the upper tiers of economic status? And do you place millionaires who have achieved their monetary success by inheritance or illegal means into the upper class merely due to their income or net worth? It quickly became apparent that, as has often been said in a metaphorical and jocular manner, "Just because an individual finds himself on third base does not necessarily mean he has hit a triple."

A 2016 Gallop poll[5] asked what determines how Americans perceive their social class, and 43 percent of those who responded identified themselves in the middle class. Social class was not well defined or well understood and was based on income, wealth, power, culture, behavior, heritage, and prestige. Only 3 percent labeled themselves as being in the upper class and 8 percent in the lower class. Interestingly, even at the lowest level of yearly household income (less than $20,000) people were equally likely to identify as lower, working, and middle class. At $40,000, individuals were more likely to say they were part of the middle class and less likely that they were in the working class. At an income of $75,000 to $99,000, those identifying as working class declined significantly, replaced by the middle class. At $150,000, upper-middle class became more prevalent along with middle class, and at $250,000 yearly income, a third of Americans identified themselves as being in the upper class, with the remaining individuals in that income bracket self-identifying as middle class. Even at more than $500,000, only half claimed that they were in the upper class, with the rest identifying themselves as being in the middle class.

Education levels made a bigger impact on how Americans classified themselves, with college-educated individuals generally viewing themselves in the upper-middle class. People aged sixty-five years and older were more likely to identify with a higher social class when compared to younger people. Race was also an influencing factor, with white individuals being more likely than non-white to identify with a higher social class. Geographic influences mattered, too, with rural individuals being less likely to identify with a higher social class when compared to those living in urban areas.

It appeared, therefore, that people often do not use their

financial status as a measure of socioeconomic class and would thus probably not measure a successful life by establishing financial achievement. Cannot someone in the lower class making $25,000 believe that they are living what they define as a successful life? The Reverend Dr. Clay Stauffer, an adjunct professor teaching a course at Vanderbilt University on "Success, Status, and the American Dream," stated that "many people have broken generational cycles of poverty to go on and achieve great things, such as J. D. Vance, who wrote *Hillbilly Elegy*."[6] And conversely, it can be said with ample anecdotal evidence that there are many in the upper class, defined as making well over $250,000, who would not consider their lives successful.

Dave Schools, a freelance editor and brand storyteller, wrote that he had always believed that money did in fact buy happiness until he attended a Yale class taught by Laura Santos, who explained to him why things we want in life do not actually make us happy.[7] She cited the 2010 Princeton survey of 450,000 Americans, which noted that while happiness does rise with one's income, the correlation peaks at about $75,000. That study is now a decade old and may not be as accurate today; however, the point stands that after a certain income that allows for the necessities of life to be available, plus a certain amount left over to enjoy other pleasures, happiness does not measurably increase. That certain amount will vary but clearly is not substantial.

Schools concluded that perhaps money does make us "a little bit happy" but that the things that do seem to make us happy include incorporating healthy habits into our lives, learning new skills, being kinder and spending money on others, making more time for friends and family, and spending less money on things that are not long-lasting. In addition, it has been reported that while real per capita income has more than tripled since the late 1950s, the percentage of people saying they are very happy has, if anything, slightly declined.[8]

Knowing this data, it seemed to me that it was more appropriate to use a different category to define a successful life than the one that measures an individual's income, net worth, or social class. Perhaps age was a better barometer, for with age comes experience, which often influences an individual's definition of success. My initial research led me to determine that age categories would be a better method to use, except when dealing with the extreme poor and intellectually challenged.

While a certain level of income may be needed for an individual to measure one's life as successful, anything less than that creates a life dedicated to survival, with the definition of a successful life being more difficult to ponder. It seemed reasonable, therefore, to ask, What about those individuals who do not earn enough income to pay for the necessities of life? What about the very poor and homeless individuals? What do they have to say about a definition of a successful life?

When one is truly poor and in the poverty class and unable to provide even the bare necessities of life, how can one attempt to address the question of success? Survival is the prominent activity that consumes life for the very poor, and the question of what defines a successful life, if it is thought about at all, is only a goal to hopefully be reached someday. In addition, a state of poverty has an overwhelming effect on one's definition of a

COME HOLY SPIRIT

OPEN The Eyes of the Blind

successful life even once that poverty has resolved, such as was the case of Rose Molduene.

When I interviewed Rose, who lives in a high-rise with her husband on the beach in Boca Raton, Florida, she helped me understand that it was what one experienced in life rather than a person's finances that helped frame the definition of a successful life. Rose, twenty-six, is a nurse and pharmaceutical representative. When I asked what she thought constituted a successful life, her response surprised me. "Having the necessities of life would define my definition of a successful life." Rose continued, "Necessities for me include steady employment so as to be able to provide shelter, three meals a day, and transportation to and from work."

Rose noted the surprised look on my face and added, "You see, years earlier in my life I was homeless and living in my car. That experience lives with me to this very day and makes me aware that it is only the bare necessities of life that truly define a successful life for me. All the other stuff is just icing on the cake." I then asked her, having attained these necessities of life, what goals did she now have that would add to her basic definition of a successful life. "To do something worthwhile, something that makes a contribution to society."

Rose provided insight into what people who live in poverty think about defining a successful life, and so I reached out to a few individuals who were living in poverty and seeking aid for shelter and nourishment for themselves and their family at Metro Social Services in Nashville. As a former commissioner of the Metro Social Services Board for ten years, I was exposed to many in Nashville who were poor and without the necessities of life. I sought out some of these individuals.

Brijan, thirty-two years old, single, and the mother of two children, ages ten and twelve, had come to Metro Social Services to obtain deposit money for a place to live. She had a car as well as a job at a restaurant downtown and had been living in a halfway house for the past three months and was now living with friends. Her life had been quite difficult. She'd spent three years in prison and was now on parole. Nevertheless, she wanted a place to live to help raise her two children. Brijan was clearly a member of the poverty class.

Brijan thought about my question for a few minutes and finally said, "A successful life is one in which I am financially stable. I want a career, not just a job. I want to be able to pay for the necessities of life, which include rent, a car, and gas for my car, car insurance, food, health care, and a cell phone. I do not want to live paycheck to paycheck, and I want to have a little extra to be able to buy things for my children. I want to start a cleaning business to help achieve these things I have listed." Then she added, "Right now my life is not successful, but I hope someday to be successful." Brijan's definition of a successful life was consistent with the premise that when one is living in significant poverty, the primary definition of a successful life would be survival. These individuals had hopes and dreams, but they were mainly concentrated on making enough money to survive.

Then I met Dan, a single thirty-two-year-old musician and artist who had been living on the streets of Nashville for the past five months. We sat down together for an interview at the

Metro Social Services one August morning in 2018. Dan was from Iowa, had obtained a GED, and had also attended college for less than a year where he had studied criminal justice and political science. Currently he was working part-time and had come to Metro Social Services to obtain money that would help him find a place to live.

Responding to my question on how he would define the elements of a successful life, Dan smiled and, looking me straight in the eye, said, "I feel successful now." He explained that for him, success was all about taking risks, and he had done that, and it had paid off. After spending time in prison, he realized as he was walking out of prison's door that he needed to take a risk and turn his life around. Dan moved from Iowa to Nashville, began painting, and was pleasantly surprised when tourists walking the streets of downtown Broadway told him that they liked his artwork, and a few actually bought his paintings. "All of a sudden, I felt successful." I pushed Dan to expand his definition of success, and so he added, "Having dreams and pushing myself to live that dream is my definition of a successful life. I am doing that now with my art and my music, and so I feel successful even now living on the street." He continued, "Money is a tool just like the acrylic for my paintings. It does not define success for me."

I asked Dan where he wanted to be in ten years, and with a clear voice and serious look on his face, he stated, "I will be at the top, and that top would be me being able to give someone a $25 Kroger gift card just as you have given me for this interview." I have learned that there are so very many definitions of a successful life, and this was just another one that allowed for a homeless man to be able to feel as if he had achieved an element of success. While he wanted more, he was content with his life as it was. He had taken risks, and it had paid off for him.

I also met Keisha at the Metro Social Services, and she was happy to be interviewed for the survey I was conducting for my book. I learned something surprising from her as well. Keisha was twenty-five years old and worked for Nashville Metro Schools as well as Walmart. She had a high-school education and was living in public housing. She was at Metro Social Services with her twenty-year-old sister to help her find housing as well. Keisha told me that she believed a successful life would be achieved "if my son, who is now seven years old, can be raised in a happy environment, and when he is an adult that he will be able to take care of himself." She added, "My son is my world, and everything I do is to make sure he is happy and well. I don't want him to be consumed with the material world, but I want him to have a roof over his head, a job, and food on his table. Then I will feel successful."

Keisha was telling me that she saw her success through the happiness and well-being of her son. Success by proxy immediately came to my mind as a means to explain her definition of a successful life. Keisha had introduced a concept for success that I eventually learned was not such a rare definition. There would be others with the same concept of success by proxy.

Jeffrey Moses, thirty-eight, was born and raised in San Diego, California, graduated from high school, and then spent half a semester at a technical college in business management.

Soon after, however, he began making some very bad decisions. Serving prison time off and on from 1993 to 2004, Jeffrey was on a very unsuccessful path. I met Jeffrey one morning at the Metro Social Services office, and he agreed to an interview. Tall and handsome, Jeffrey was articulate and thoughtful. His responses to my questions were clear, concise, and open. I could tell that his life had not been an easy one.

After moving to Nashville in 2004, Jeffrey was paroled and did not return to a life of crime. He was not working when we met; he'd lost a job at a local fast-food restaurant and was now seeking aid to feed his family. Divorced, Jeffrey had five children ages twenty months to ten years old, and he was the sole parent for all five, as his ex-wife was uninvolved with the children. Renting an apartment with government vouchers, Jeffrey spent much of each day making sure his children were taken care of, attended school, and had a parent who loved them. His sister helped him with some of these activities, but basically, he was alone. He was the sole provider, protector, and parent. But he also had several volunteer jobs. He volunteered at his children's school, was on a policy committee for an Early Head Start program, and served on the board for a ministry in town and on an advisory board oversight committee for a homeless shelter in Nashville. He was looking for a job that would allow him to be a parent as well as to continue his volunteer work, and that was not easy. He was at the Metro Social Services Department the morning we met seeking assistance. I asked him, what was his definition of a successful life?

"A successful life is one in which you deal with the real pains of life and are able to come out the other side in a positive way and that you have taken something of value from those experiences. I feel both good and not good where I am now because I have made errors along the way and need to be further along than I am at this time in my life. My next step to feel real success will be being able to help others. My success is a team effort. All successful people have had help and encouragement. No one does it all by themselves."

Jeffrey then added, "In many ways I feel successful now, because I am no longer homeless, and my kids have a place to call their own. I want to be part of a system that helps people by volunteering my time to achieve these goals. To sum it up, I have the feeling of success right now for a variety of reasons. First, I have been able to stay out of prison; I am taking good care of my five kids; I am volunteering to help others in need; and I am working with others who are helping me. But I have a long way to go to feel the ultimate feeling of success, which will include helping others in need. That is my real passion."

Nashonda Milan was thirty-nine years old when I interviewed her at the Metro Social Services office. Nashonda was born and raised in Nashville, graduated from high school, and then studied nursing for a year and a half. She had to leave nursing school due to social reasons and told me that she regrets not finishing her studies but that it was never too late to return. She has never been married and has six children from two different partners and for the past eight months had been living in her truck with her children ages six to thirteen. She worked part-time at a security firm. Life was quite difficult for this pleasant young woman who was at Metro Social Services in hopes of getting an apartment to live in. "A successful life to me is to know that I have never given up and that I have been a strong woman as well as a good example for my kids. I want to be consistent in achieving my goals." When I asked her what her goals were, she responded by saying that she wanted to begin working full-time, pay off her student loans so she can return to nursing school, get married, and then be able to live in a nice house with a picket fence and garden. "Right now, however, I am just trying to survive."

I also met Stanley Walker at the Metro Social Services office the same day I interviewed Nashonda Milan. Stanley was fifty-nine years old at the time of the interview, and I found him to be very interesting. Stanley was born and raised on a farm in West Tennessee. His father was a dentist and owned several farms. After graduating from high school, Stanley worked on one of the farms for many years. He never married nor had any children. Unfortunately, Stanley got involved with cocaine and spent thirty months in a Tennessee prison before being released at age forty-nine. He told me that he was "dumped" in Nashville after being released and began living at Room at the Inn, a homeless shelter in Nashville. For the past four years, he has been living in an apartment paid for by Supplemental Security Income. He told me that prison saved his life by helping him understand that he needed to change his way of living. While attempting to be employed, Stanley had a heart attack, and because of his health has not been able to work.

When I asked for his definition, much like Dan, he told me, "I have had a wonderful life, and so many people have been so wonderful to me and have given me so much help. The problems I have had have all been my fault, and I take full responsibilities for my actions. I have enjoyed my life and have learned to take the bad with the good. A successful life is waking up every day being happy with what I have. I am a grateful man; I tell the truth and am very happy with my life."

After interviewing these individuals who were or had been living a life of survival, I came away with several important conclusions. It was necessary to have reached out to these few individuals who were living in poverty or near poverty as their definitions were different in some ways and similar in others from the lives of those who had reached levels of income to afford the necessities of life. It became obvious that so much of an individual's definition of a successful life is dependent on what that individual has experienced. Rose could not separate her definition from the fact that for six months of her early life she was homeless. Brijan's only thought was to get out of poverty and begin to pay for the necessities of life. Success for her would be when she reached that goal. Jeffrey also couldn't separate his definition of success from his experiences of jail, poverty, and parenthood and felt that in many ways he had a long way to go to be successful.

Then there was the surprise elicited upon interviewing Dan and Stanley. Even though both clearly had lived difficult lives and were still living lives of poverty, Dan believed he was already living a successful life, because to him success was being able to sell his paintings on the streets of Nashville, and Stanley told me he has had a wonderful life despite all the downs he has encountered.

Keisha added something I had not considered: the concept of success by proxy. Though living in poverty and struggling to make ends meet, her definition was focused on her son's success in life. If he was successful by her minimalist criteria, then she would feel as if her life had been a successful one. Success by proxy would be a new item on the long list of definitions I was to encounter in my research for this book and would also become a consideration for one of my definitions as well. Already it had become apparent that our concept of a successful life revolves around our life experiences, choices, and goals. So much for a simple definition of what constitutes a successful life!

There was another group that I wanted to reach out to as well. These were individuals with intellectual disabilities. I believed that these unique individuals could not be placed in a category of socioeconomic class or age as their disabilities often created an environment that would result in a different perspective on the definition of a successful life. I was particularly interested in a few individuals who were born with Down syndrome as my grandson, Seth, now sixteen years old, was born with this diagnosis. I believed individuals with Down syndrome, and other intellectual disabilities would give me a different perspective on my question of what constitutes a successful life.

Will McMillan is thirty-one years old, born with a diagnosis of Down syndrome. I went to his home in Nashville one fall day and sat with him and his father, Tom, to get his definition of a successful life. It was a most interesting visit. Will is high-functioning, and after listening to his accomplishments and activities I was very impressed with all he has been able to do. Will was mainstreamed in both public and private schools, earning a high-school diploma, and then spent two years at a Vanderbilt University program equivalent to a college experience. Currently, Will has part-time jobs at two YMCA sites in Nashville as well as at an agency working on the behalf of the intellectually disabled in Tennessee, but he does so much more. He swims, plays basketball, is a fourth-degree black belt in Tae kwon do, attends two book clubs, and hangs out with friends at various Nashville parks.

Will lives by himself five days of the week in Friendship House apartments, where people with disabilities and Vanderbilt divinity students live in a community, but he lives with his parents on the weekend for his time to wash his clothes, attend church services and sporting events, and do his grocery shopping. He does not drive a car. He has a good memory and a sense of humor, as well as a pleasant smile and personality. We finally got around to his definition of a successful life. "To me success is enjoying what I have, which are the good memories of the moments I have with my family and friends. I like being who I am, and I have good friends." Will did not add more to this definition. To him, the moments he shares with his loving family and good friends and the memories that come from those moments are what makes his life successful.

"It doesn't bother me that I have Down syndrome." These words were some of the first words spoken to me when I went to interview Brett Wolf, a thirty-five-year-old young man from Texas who lives in a group home in Austin with ninety other individuals with disabilities and who also told me, "I am proud of myself for living on my own, and that makes me feel successful." Brett was born and raised in Texas, graduated from high school, and then worked for his father for a long time. Currently he has two jobs, one at Whole Foods corporate offices and one at a real estate firm where he works in the mail room, brings coffee to employees, and is a general office worker. Brett likes to exercise, likes to go bowling (he was in the Special Olympics competing in bowling), and likes hanging out with his friends and family.

"A successful life for me is to be with my friends and family." He is very close with his parents as well as his younger brother, sister-in-law, and several uncles and aunts. They make him happy. Brett is high-functioning and clearly able to do much on his own. He Ubers to concerts, movies, and synagogue, became a Bar Mitzvah at the age of thirteen, went to a summer camp for five years, and even travels some on his own. When asked what disabilities he has, Brett mentioned his stuttering speech but otherwise felt good about himself. Brett is a very charming and friendly young man who believes that he is successful because he has a loving family and friends and, very importantly, because he is able to live independently. His last words to me as we ended the interview were as interesting as his first. "I feel very proud of myself."

I met Ivan Weinstein when we were both teenagers. It was obvious to me and the other boys and girls in my class in junior high school that Ivan was different. In those days, there were not the large number of diagnoses that pervade our culture today, and so we just accepted Ivan, knowing he had some aspect of intellectual disability. I wanted Ivan to tell me his definition of a successful life. Ivan is now seventy-eight years old, and we see each other quite often as he is a member of the same synagogue I attend. He told me that for him, a successful life was one in which he was able to be employed and to take care of himself after his parents both died. "In spite of the fact that I had to be in special education, I eventually got a job working for the Tennessee State Government as a typist for thirty-six years, and I have been living on my own for a long time." Success for Ivan is focused on quite specific goals. Getting a job and being able to take care of himself and living alone were the definitions of his success.

James Presley is thirty-five years old and was diagnosed with intellectual disability as a young boy. He was able to graduate from high school and now lives in Stewart Home School in Frankfort, Kentucky. The home houses approximately 220 individuals with a variety of intellectual issues, with 40 percent of the residents diagnosed with Down syndrome. James does not have a job but spends his time doing chores around his dormitory, attending educational classes, painting, singing in a choir, playing basketball and soccer, and occasionally fishing in a pond on the property. "Success to me is to be able to comb my hair, brush my teeth, shave, and be able to take care of myself, as well as to take care of my room. I also like being with my friends and family." When I asked him if he felt successful, he smiled and said, "I feel successful now."

•

Over the years I developed a philosophy that has helped me place life's unfolding events into perspective. It is not how one begins in life, but rather how one finishes that is truly important.

Born into this world, we mortals are blueprints of our parents, totally dependent on caretakers for sustenance and survival. Helpless and unaware, we are ushered into childhood where, for the most part, we can make few decisions about our environment and surroundings. Slowly but surely, we dip our toes into the river of adolescence, finding currents of change and turbulence. It is here that we finally understand the feeling of individuality. While at this stage, we yearn for independence and freedom but find that our parents, teachers, and other supervisors are still watching over us with increased vigor, attempting to fine-tune these important years of growth.

The final years of high school and then beyond give us the freedom and independence we have sought, only to reveal that often we do not know what we really want. These early years of independence are a time when we are shaped and molded by external factors and circumstances. As we enter the third decade of our lives, we begin to have the opportunity to make decisions that are life-changing. We are, in essence, becoming the sum total of our choices; however, when we are young and inexperienced, we are more prone to making errors that can also be life-altering. Choosing the wrong lifestyle, profession, or spouse are only a few of the mistakes we occasionally make. Some of us make these mistakes on a repetitive basis, but when we are young, society seems to overlook many of our mistakes with a blanket "been there, done that" attitude, and we are given time and more opportunities to get it right.

As we enter the fourth and fifth decades of our lives, we seem to get more things right, and it is just in the nick of time.

When we reach this age, society is less accepting of mistakes that were once excused when we were young. At this stage in our lives, an increasing level of maturity and wisdom begins to develop, and opportunities narrow. Making the correct choices becomes more critical in shaping who we are and how we are eventually going to live our lives.

It is during the last few decades of our lives when having loving relationships with family and friends, being satisfied with the work we have done, and feeling as if we have made a difference seem to matter most. These later years determine how each of us will eventually be remembered, because as was said, it is not how you start your life but how you finish it.

As we age, much more affects our ability to feel as if our lives have been meaningful and successful. In general, according to a 2010 Gallup poll, when we are young, we feel pretty good about ourselves.[9] As time progresses, however, we tend to lose much of our euphoria as we encounter responsibilities of work, making a living, being married, raising children, and dealing with many of the complexities of life. The incidence of being worried about something in life tends to remain stable until around fifty years of age, at which time being worried begins to slowly decline. The authors of this Gallup poll noted that factors such as whether one had a partner or a job, was male or female, or had children at home did not make a difference.

I believe this increasing happiness is closely related to aging simply because as we grow older, we gain wisdom, and it is that wisdom that makes us happier. Over the years we learn what brings us pleasure and what has the opposite effect. For example, we understand that a seductive ad in a magazine portraying a young couple in a hammock on a beautiful beach while holding a tropical drink is not what it appears to be. We ask basic questions such as, where does the couple place their drinks, how comfortable is it really for two people to share a hammock, how hot is the sand, where are other people to mingle with, what does the room in the hotel look like, how difficult is it to travel to this place, and does it have internet access? We might have succumbed to this ad at an earlier age but now understand that to travel to this "beach paradise" may not actually bring us pleasure or happiness. We understand better what is truly important to us and what is not. We are experienced and therefore have attained increasing wisdom.

As we age, we also begin to accept who we are and what life still has in store for us. We understand that while we may not attain certain dreams or desires, this is not necessarily a bad thing. We instinctively know what we have accomplished at work or in our family and personal life and find increasing pleasure knowing that much of this experience has been rewarding and good. Our increasing wisdom allows us to better understand what life is about and what role we play in it.

We learn that it is more important for us to smell the flowers and follow the rule of "be here now, now be here." It has been said that our days are like scrolls and that we should write on them only what we want remembered. As we age, it becomes imperative that we live our lives in such a manner that those we leave behind someday will remember us as kind, compassionate, honest, ethical, and loving.

Time seems to move more quickly as we reach our golden years, much as a rewinding tape moves slowly at first and then more rapidly as it nears the end. If, however, we enhance our days with awareness, fulfillment, integrity, and love, then when the passage of our time comes to an end, those who knew and loved us will know we lived our lives well and that our time on earth was spent wisely.

CHAPTER 2

THE YOUNG

"Follow your heart but take your brain with you." Alfred Adler

"The surest way to be happy is to seek happiness for others." Eleanor Roosevelt

"Success is not the key to happiness; happiness is the key to success." Albert Schweitzer

"Happiness is a butterfly: the more you chase it, the more it flies away from you and hides. But stop chasing it, put away your net and busy yourself with other, more productive things than the pursuit of personal happiness, and it will sneak up on you from behind and perch on your shoulder." Rabbi Harold Kushner

"Youth is not a time of life; it is a state of mind." Samuel Ullman

"People can discover their greatest qualities in the moment of their greatest need." Walt Whitman

ASKING YOUNG INDIVIDUALS RANGING IN AGE from fourteen to twenty-four how they would define a successful life might seem unfair. Without many experiences to help determine what the important aspects of feeling successful are, you may think their responses would be sophomoric or simplistic. From my interviews with many young individuals, nothing could be further from the truth. Although they may have had less experience, when reaching out to teenagers and individuals in their early twenties, I found these young people who were just beginning to think about what they wanted to do with their lives were nonetheless able to express considerable nuances in their responses.

I began my interviews with my granddaughter, Marly, who at the time was a mature and intelligent fourteen-year-old eighth-grade homeschooled student in Chicago. When asked her definition of a successful life, she responded with the following: "A successful life is one in which you help change the world to make it a better place in some way or another and to help others along the way in their journey through life. A successful life also means you have been able to use whatever gift God has given you in the most productive manner." Marly's answer belied her young age and lack of a long life of varied experiences.

Being trained in the world of academics, I am often reminded that the plural of *anecdote* is not *data*, so to reach a larger diverse group of teens I asked a leader of teenagers in Boca Raton, Florida, to obtain her students' definition of a successful life. I wanted to hear their thoughts on a subject that they probably had not yet considered. Here are some of their written responses:

"A successful life is when a person lives happy, doing what they love to do." Derek, 18

"Happiness is the one thing needed for a successful life. Friends and money are all just accessories in our lifestyles, but if we are not happy through it all, it is meaningless." Jordon, 17

"A successful life is all about happiness and not money, not cars, just happiness." Amari, 18

"I think a successful life is measured by how happy you can make others feel, how strongly you can love, and how authentic are the things you create. Success cannot really be defined materially, rather it is how fulfilled you let yourself be." Alexis, 19

"I believe what makes life successful is finding what you love to do and what you are passionate about and never giving up on that search. It is about finding what makes you happy and putting everything you have into it no matter what anyone else says." Emily, 17

"Success is when you are happy with your life and you do not have to stress out about paying bills. If you have children, they are smart and respectful. Not everyone can be successful." Nicole, 17

"To have a successful life means to be able to make yourself and the people you love happy." Huyen, 18

"To me, a successful life is not about money or power, but about happiness. Finding things you are passionate about and finding love creates a successful life." Nema, 18

"A successful life includes being happy with relationships and being stable with your money." Ben, 17

"A successful life consists of happiness and having a drive to become a better person than you are at every moment of your life." Arrayo, 17

"A successful life is when the person feels happy and accomplished. The person should be comfortable and happy with their position in life. As long as they enjoy their lives, they are successful." Miller, 17

"A life filled with happiness and comfort is a successful life. This can be achieved by forming deep personal bonds with people and finding pride in your career." Jabez, 17

"A successful life comes through happiness and giving back to others." Engg, 17

"What makes a successful life is being happy with your life despite shortcomings and obstacles." Asia, 17

I listed these fourteen high-school students together, as they each cited happiness as a significant factor in living a successful life. While the state of happiness is quite difficult to define, these teenagers felt that happiness was of utmost importance. Some mentioned other factors, such as having a career and loving what you do, being content with what you have done, forming deep personal bonds with people, having enough money so not to be stressed, and giving back to others. But, for most of these teenagers, being happy was the predominate answer to attaining a successful life.

There were other teenagers, such as my granddaughter, who did not mention the word *happiness* in their definition. A strong-willed eighteen-year-old student, Mikyal, stated, "What makes a successful life is not backing down in the face of adversity."

I also had varying answers from the numerous seventeen-year-old students who told me of their definition. John, a dreamer, wrote, "Follow your dream and use what you are good at, stay with your beliefs, stand your ground, and don't let anyone get you off of your focus." Jacobe had this to say: "A successful life is being able to fulfill your dreams and accomplish the things you wanted to accomplish." Lauren wrote, "A successful life is when you have been able to do what you are passionate about doing." Alexandria said, "A successful life is when you have the motivation and courage to keep trying and never give up. You must continue to work hard and never stop, as your work is never done because there is always something that needs to be done."

Emma felt, "You need to have a plan for your life, a plan to graduate college and be involved throughout your community. You also need to be prepared for the hard times in life that await you." Benjamin wrote, "A successful life demands drive, focus, pursuing goals, responding to obstacles with motivation and perseverance rather than with despondence."

On a practical note, Priya said, "A successful life is one in which you have enough money to sustain a comfortable lifestyle." Equally practical, Dana stated that "a successful life is determined by how financially stable you are and that you love the career you are in."

Jacob got down to some other basics when he said that "a successful life is having a family that you love," but then the seventeen-year-old added, "as well as having a college education and a successful career." Brittni determined that "a successful life is one where you've worked hard for what you have and are content with where you are and the people around you."

While these teenagers did not mention being happy, they did include a variant of other important definitions including loving what you do, having enough money to live a comfortable life, not backing down from adversity, following your dreams, having a loving family, having a college education, and responding to obstacles with perseverance.

Next, I reached out to four Vanderbilt University students one spring day on the Vanderbilt campus. These four young men in their early twenties appeared eager to meet with me. When we met at their Zeta Beta Tau fraternity house one evening, they did not hesitate to express their opinions on what they considered to be the definition of a successful life.

Louis Schatzki, twenty years old and a junior at Vanderbilt from Lexington, Kentucky, majoring in physics, responded to my question by stating, "A successful life for me relates to my career aspirations. I want to do something that advances human nature and to make a contribution that helps the progress of human beings. I am career-focused, and if I succeed in that goal, I will consider my life successful." And then he added, "I am sure that definition of a successful life will change over time, but at this time in my life, a successful life is centered in knowing that I have helped advance human knowledge."

Twenty-one-year-old senior Owen Averbuch, from Huntsville, Alabama, was majoring in human organization and development. Answering my question with a warm demeanor and friendly smile, he said, "A successful life has changed for me. When I was younger, I just wanted to be rich, and that was about it. Now, however, it will mean that I have had a positive career in the business of real estate, which is what I plan to do after graduation. It will also mean that I have made good decisions, invested my time and resources well, and made good friends along the way and that I have had a big and close family. Basically, I want to contribute to society both politically as well as philanthropically. If I can do all this, I will feel that my life has been a successful one."

Joe Ferber, twenty years old and a junior from Northbrook, Chicago, was majoring in neuroscience and psychology and wants to be a physician. "When I look back on my life, I want to be able to say that I had few regrets and that I lived an honest, embracing, ethical, and moral life. No regrets for me means that I was a good physician, took good care of my patients, and had a good reputation. I will probably have some regrets; however, I want those to be small ones, not life-altering, and most importantly, I want to have learned from each of them. At this stage in my life, I am not sure how family and money will be a part of my definition of a successful life. It may be a big part of my definition someday, or it may not be."

Finally, there was twenty-year-old Max Schneider, a junior from New York City majoring in political science and communication and interested in sports journalism. A successful life to Max will also change over time, but he stated that he wants to be happy in what he is doing and that he wants to have left behind a legacy. That will be an important part of his definition of happiness. "My greatest fear is that I will be forgotten." When pressed on his definition of happiness, he responded, "Happiness is knowing you have had a positive effect on the lives of others."

I wanted to interview more college students, so I reached out to students on the Vanderbilt campus. I met twenty-one-year-old Emily O'Brian one day when I lectured to a Vanderbilt University undergraduate class on the subject of narrative medicine. I asked for her definition of a successful life, and she said she wanted to think about it and send it to me via email. Here is what she wrote: "I would define a successful life as a life in which I am doing what makes me feel most fulfilled while being surrounded by the people I love most. And I hope that through this my life would reflect the life of Jesus Christ, so that his light can shine in the darkness of the world."

Another Vanderbilt University undergraduate student in the narrative medicine class also sent me an email with her definition. Rebecca Brisman, age twenty-one, wrote, "I believe a successful life is defined by the positive impact that one has on others. I will feel fulfilled if I leave the world a better place than when I got here, while hopefully finding the time to explore my passions and surround myself with love along the way."

In the fall of 2019, I lectured to another undergraduate class at Vanderbilt University entitled "Success, Status and the American Dream" and requested that each of the students in attendance send me their definition of a successful life. I believed this group who was studying the very subject I was writing a book about would be illuminating.

Nineteen-year-old Sahanya Bhaktaram wrote, "Living a

successful life means feeling good with who you are as a person, having reciprocal relationships with people you love and trust, finding something that motivates you, and knowing when to push yourself and when to relax. There is always something to be grateful for, and there is always something to work for. Perhaps that is how to feel successful; being grateful, but never settled."

Gracie Gumm was eighteen years old and summed up her definition with, "To live a successful life means to live a life that you can be proud of. What you can be proud of can mean many different things; however, a good indicator of being proud would be what the impact of the work you are doing has on the well-being of society."

Jessica Prus, who was nineteen years old, had this to say: "A successful life would be a balance between vocation, relationships, and economic stability." And Spencer Brents, who was twenty-one, wrote, "Success should be understood as a deeply personal and internal concept. A state of being or perpetual condition marked by contentment and happiness should be considered success and should be understood in terms of the strength of one's relationships, the fulfillment of one's endeavors, and the peacefulness of one's self-understanding."

Cooper Sean Long, nineteen, had a most interesting definition of a successful life. "I feel successful in life when I fall asleep easily without the hypothetical future on my mind." Cooper's only definition centered on a state where he was not hindered by worries of his future.

Ilana Wolchinsky, age nineteen, wrote, "The key to a successful life is to identify your values and support them behaviorally.

As a result, happiness will follow. Giving back to one's community and impacting a future generation allows your success to go beyond what you could ever do."

Lindsay Quackenbush, who was twenty-two years old, stated that "a successful life means feeling at ease and balanced in the world. This would include having a network of friends who I can confide in and will support me when I need it, maintaining and growing my relationships with everyone in my family and always making time for them, having a meaningful job that excites me and provides a salary that supports my desired lifestyle, and feeling as though what I do makes the world a better place."

Jacob Passalaqua, age eighteen, wrote that "success is the act of balancing financial independence and sustainability with meaningful contribution to the family as well as the larger community." Claire Hagney, age twenty-one, wrote, "A successful life is one in which you feel as though you have helped as many people as possible and formed meaningful and deep relationships."

Eva Burchholz, who was twenty-one years old, wrote, "Life is not all smiles and sunshine, but a successful person has the resilience to bounce back from setbacks and lives an unselfish life helping to improve the lives of others."

Joel Decoursey, age eighteen, wrote that "a successful life is having a job that I enjoy going to every day, having a wife who I love and enjoy spending time with, having a house in a nice neighborhood where I can raise children, and finally, leaving those around me better than when I first met them." Toleafoa McMoore, age twenty-one, wrote, "My definition of success in life is being satisfied with my actions in life, having wealth from a job I love, and lastly marrying my soulmate."

These young individuals, which included high-school teenagers and college-aged students, centered their definition of a successful life around several disparate definitions, with happiness being the most frequently mentioned. Also, loving the career you have chosen, making a positive impact on the lives of others, and having love in your life were the next most frequently mentioned. Following these definitions in order of frequency were having enough money to live as you wish, handling adversity, following your dreams, and making good friends.

Several of these young individuals also mentioned having smart and respectful children, making others happy, being educated, striving to be a better person, having few regrets, living a moral and ethical life, and being grateful. These young individuals have tasted little of life's experiences and, therefore, their focus on happiness and developing a skill that would allow them to feel productive and needed was not surprising; however, many mentioned other significant and important goals they wished to achieve.

Being happy was another of the most often-quoted important elements of a successful life, which made me wonder, what exactly defines a state of happiness? Over the years I have been fascinated with the concept of happiness and what it means. Our Founding Fathers felt this human condition was so important that they added it into the Declaration of Independence in 1776: "We hold these truths to be self-evident, that all men are created equal, that they are endowed by their Creator with certain unalienable Rights, that among these are Life, Liberty and the pursuit of Happiness." Happiness means different things to different people, and the answer to the question "are you happy?" obviously depends on many different factors.

Using over forty years of extensive research on the subject of happiness, social scientists have identified three major sources: genes, events, and values. Researchers at the University of Minnesota have tracked many identical twins who were separated at birth and raised in different environments and found that it is our genetic wiring that accounts for almost half of our state of happiness.[10] To a large degree, therefore, fundamentally happy or unhappy individuals get it honestly from their parents. Arthur C. Brooks, an American social scientist, has also stated that happiness is 50 percent genetics—or the way we are wired—and 50 percent how life plays out.[11]

Studies have also revealed that isolated events in our lives have a big impact on our state of happiness, with the only problem being that the effects are usually short-lived. A pay raise or new job or reaching a major milestone in life can certainly bring happiness, yet time dulls so many of these events. It appears the quest and hard work to attain a lofty goal may bring more happiness than the actual achievement of that goal.

The third process involved in bringing happiness into one's life is that of values involving faith, family, and friendships. Having a foundation of spiritual support, a close and loving family, and many dear friends can be a major source of bringing happiness into one's life. This should not be surprising.

What is surprising, however, is that research has shown that satisfaction of work, regardless of income, is a major determinant of a person's state of happiness. The University of Chicago has, since 1972, conducted a survey of Americans about happiness and found that more than 80 percent claim they were either completely satisfied, very satisfied, or fairly satisfied with their work and that this finding held across educational and income levels.[12]

There is a level of income below which Americans are so focused on survival it is difficult for them to achieve a state of happiness. Brooks, who is also president of the American Enterprise Institute, wrote in the *New York Times*, "Relieving poverty brings big happiness, but income, per se, does not." He also notes that "work can bring happiness by marrying our passions to our skills, empowering us to create value in our lives and in the lives of others."[13] All this would help explain why so many Americans respond positively when asked about their state of happiness.

Why is it that an increase in prosperity does not necessarily bring an increase of happiness? Jonathan Rauch, writing in the *New York Times*, noted that "in America and also in other countries, an impressive rise in material well-being had zero effect in personal well-being." It seems that happiness is relative. We tend to compare ourselves to others, and as Gore Vidal has said, "It is not enough for me to succeed; others must fail."[14] In other words, when others succeed by making more money, this may decrease our happiness level. We humans are a competitive group, and despite doing well in life's measure of success, when those we live with do better, we lose a sense of our own happiness level.

It appears, therefore, that since money above a certain level does not bring or even increase happiness in our lives, we can be reassured that if we encourage our children to educate themselves and find employment they enjoy that will allow for a reasonable but not necessarily large income, they will answer yes when asked if they are happy.

From a definitional point of view, happiness, viewed as a persistent and long-lasting feeling of contentment, is regulated by serotonin, a powerful neurotransmitter found especially in the brain and blood. Perhaps many confuse the state of happiness with that of pleasure. Happiness and pleasure are different. Pleasure is an episodic state of increased euphoria mediated by another neurotransmitter, dopamine, which is considered to be the underlying cause of addiction and according to Robert Lustig, an endocrinologist, "makes the brain say, 'this is good, I want more.' Happiness, on the other hand, regulated and mediated by serotonin, is not addictive, is long term, and makes the brain say, 'this feels good and it is enough.'"[15]

In his book *When Bad Things Happen to Good People*, Rabbi Harold Kushner writes the following: "The happiest people you know are probably not the richest or most famous, probably not the ones who work hardest at being happy by reading the articles and buying the books and latching on to the latest fads. I suspect that the happiest people you know are the ones who work at being kind, helpful, and reliable, and happiness sneaks into their lives while they are busy doing these things. You don't become happy by pursuing happiness. It is always a by-product, never a primary goal."[16]

In Nebraska senator Ben Sasse's book *Them,* the senator raises the issue of loneliness as a major cause of a state of unhappiness. "As reams of research now show, we're richer and better informed and more connected and unhappier and more isolated and less fulfilled." Sasse notes that Americans are suffering from an increase of loneliness. "A fifth of Americans volunteer that loneliness is a major source of unhappiness in their lives, and a full third of those over the age of 45 confess that chronic loneliness is a fundamental challenge with which they are struggling."[17]

Sasse gives a prescription on how to be happy based on social scientists who have identified four primary drivers of human happiness, which can be put into the form of four questions:

1. Do you have family you love and who love you?

2. Do you have friends you trust and confide in?

3. Do you have work that matters—callings that benefit your neighbors?

4. Do you have a worldview that can make sense of suffering and death?

Young people who are just beginning to think about what they want to do with their lives define a successful life in a less experienced manner. These young individuals often have not been able to experience enough of what life has to offer to be able to discern what it is to live a truly successful life. And yet, as I read each of their comments, I see that these young individuals offered numerous definitions that seemed to belie their youth, with the top two definitions being happiness and making a positive impact on the lives of others, closely followed by having a job or career they enjoyed. They also mentioned, in order of decreasing frequency, making money, having a loving family and good friends, finding love, handling adversity, following your dreams, having a plan, being content with your life, becoming a better person, having smart and respectful children, properly using the gifts God has given you, having few regrets, living a moral and ethical life, reflecting a life of Christ, being grateful, and having a life of which you can be proud. Clearly, these are other very basic aspects of living a life of success.

As we age and gain more experience and spend more time contemplating the meaning of life, we spread our wings and delve into a more nuanced definition, as we shall see in later chapters. Nonetheless, it is impressive that these young individuals were able to articulate what they considered to be the important ingredients of a successful life. Determining if they have fulfilled their definitions will come later in life. More of our young adults should attempt to contemplate their definitions as they begin their hopefully long journey of life.

CHAPTER 3

THE MATURING AGE

"We need to recognize that it is human nature to be flawed." David Brooks

"Love and work: Those are the two items that together create a worthy human being." Anne Bernays

"The biggest risk of all is taking no risk at all." Mark Alan Barnett, songwriter

"Our proper business in life is not to accumulate large fortunes, not to gain high honors and important offices in the State, but constantly to improve ourselves in habits of piety and virtue." John Adams

"Blessed is the influence of one true, loving human soul upon another." George Eliot

ONCE THE TEENAGE YEARS AND EARLY TWENTIES
are behind us and we move into our mid- to late twenties, a certain level of maturity has been infused into our lives, thanks to the life experiences we universally encounter. In the two and a half decades from our mid-twenties to fifty years of age, there are enough experiences to guide us to a more refined "good judgment" phase in our lives. We have lived long enough and suffered through countless events that help define how we think and act. I was curious how this age group would define a successful life. The definition of a life well lived would naturally change not only as we age but more importantly as we experience the many ups and downs that accompany the aging process.

Marcel Rivers, twenty-eight years old, married, with three children, is a social worker with a master's degree in public administration. He highlighted this concept of a changing definition of a successful life as we age. "When I was a teenager, I did not think much about success other than whether or not I was able to purchase the coolest tennis shoes or participate well in sports. But then I got into trouble with the law and realized that I needed to get my act together, which I did. I got into a college, and for the first time in my life, I thought about success and what I needed to do to be successful. I realized that I needed to do well and graduate college. That was my new definition of success, and I achieved it. I got my college degree. Now I needed to get a job and make money. This was my new definition of success, and once again I achieved my goal."

Marcel had a calm demeanor and a soft voice that spoke with a refreshing level of maturity. Clearly, Marcel had thought much about the question I posed to him. "When I was twenty-one years old, my daughter was born, and suddenly my definition of success changed once again. I thought success was being able to take care of my daughter and wife, which meant being able to pay for all the necessities of life for my small family. At age twenty-eight, I am looking at the bigger picture. Success now means having more than just the necessities of life. I wanted more to be successful. I wanted to own my own house, drive a car that I owned without car notes, and finally be putting money aside for my family in the years ahead, and as before, I have now achieved that goal as well."

He continued, "My final goal to be successful is to be able to say that I made a positive difference in other people's lives. Being a social worker will help me be able to someday say exactly that." Marcel, although not even thirty, clearly saw how his definition of success had already changed and would continue to change as he grew older and had more experiences and responsibilities. He is not alone in having this evolving and changing definition of a successful life.

Jeff Sonsino is forty-four years old and an optometrist. I met him several years ago when he worked at Vanderbilt University Medical Center. He graciously agreed to spend an hour with me one Sunday morning at his home. Jeff was born and raised in Philadelphia and trained in Chicago before moving to Nashville. He is married and the father of two children. He is extremely passionate about the work he performs and clearly is an entre-preneur in his field, having obtained numerous patents as well as several prestigious awards for his work in optometry. Currently he is cofounder and chief medical officer of a contact lens com-pany and spends half his time in this role and the other 50 per-cent in his private practice seeing patients. "A successful life to me," he offered, "is one where I can go to sleep at night and feel good about the decisions I made that day and the help I have given to my patients. I feel successful if when I wake up in the morning, I can look forward to being useful in the hours ahead. That usefulness translates into doing good things for my patients and bucking the system that often does not have the best interest of patients in mind."

After I explained my objective definition of a successful life to Jeff, he responded that he would agree that he had been able to minimize his negative genetic and environmental influences and was, therefore, successful by that definition. He had been born with significant scoliosis of his spine, which kept him from athletic endeavors and gave him an appearance that he felt was not "good-looking," so Jeff felt traumatized as a child. He felt ordinary. Somehow, however, Jeff began to realize he had other talents, and after attracting a beautiful young woman to become his wife and having two healthy and wonderful children, his self-esteem blossomed. "I am no longer ordinary; I matter and want to continue to matter in making a real difference in the lives of my patients and my family."

PJ Pearse is twenty-five years old and co-owner, along with his father, of a cigar store in Nashville and a very thoughtful young man. He is a graduate of Belmont University in Nashville and engaged to be married. "A successful life is defined by happiness. The adventure of life is seeking and attaining happiness, with happiness being defined by enjoying what you do and what you have done." PJ added a slight caveat: "What makes you happy changes over the years, so my definition of what makes me happy now will change as I age." PJ's definition is not dissimilar from many young individuals listed in the previous chapter. He is very aware, however, of the fact that what will make him happy today will most likely change as he gets older.

I asked my thirty-four-year-old niece, Jennifer Goldstein, who was in the process of getting a master's degree in the field of social science, to give me her definition. Jennifer and I are very close with a loving relationship. She is intelligent and mature beyond her age, with a beautiful smile and disposition. What she told me did not surprise me. "A successful life is to know that I left this world a little better than when I entered it. That could be making societal changes or treating people with kindness and respect, to be someone who brings about more smiles than tears and to continue to think clearly and be open to what life offers me."

Sarah Johnson, age thirty-five, a senior administrator in a medical office, had this to say in response to my question: "A successful life is when you are not afraid to die. Adults have a heightened awareness of the unknown, and often live by the 'should have, could have, and would have' game of life; however, if an adult is facing death, and they have an inner peace on leaving this world, they have had a successful life." Clearly, her definition focused on one fragment of life's events: that of death.

I was interested in interviewing a member of our Nashville police force and was able to sit down with Master Patrol Officer David Wright with the Belle Meade Police Department. David was thirty-seven years old, married, with a two-year-old son. He was gregarious with a very pleasing personality and smile. He has been a police officer for the past fifteen years and had several episodes as a policeman of which he was quite proud. His first response to my question of what his definition of a successful life is was, "I am not at the top of a mountain, but I like where I am now. I am a good cop, and that is what I strive for. I have had my moments of success in my career in which I made a difference in the outcome of criminal activity, but that is not all. I want to move up the career ladder and be more financially secure; however, I will not feel a failure if I am unable to move upward. Success to me is to be the best cop I can be and to live a moral and ethical life in my work and at home."

A forty-four-year-old social worker, Wandria Webb, answered my question with a succinct statement. "For me, a successful life means doing what you love for a living, maintaining healthy relationships with friends and family, and being in the best physical health possible."

Andrew Shafer is thirty-seven years old, married, and the father of five children. He works in the developmental office at the Nashville Symphony. After an initial discussion about the financial health of our wonderful Nashville Symphony, I moved to the subject at hand, regarding his definition of a successful life. "A successful life to me is when I have achieved the goal of balancing a life between my family and my career. When you have a family, you think more about what it takes to be successful. Now that I have a family, I will consider my life successful if I believe that I had been present in the lives of my children and at the same time present in my chosen career."

Jill Slamon is thirty-eight years old, married, with two children. She's a genetic counselor at Vanderbilt University Medical Center. Jill's definition is, "Having the choice to do what I want with my time and energy." Jill told me that she has worked very hard to get where she is today but understands that she has also been given a lot of opportunities to create a life for herself that is solely of her choosing. "Many people are not afforded the privilege and opportunity to pursue their dreams and therefore have less choice in their lives." Jill believes that because she has been able to live out her dreams of doing the kind of work she loves and having a family with her wife and two children, she is living a life that she considers successful.

Diego Nino is forty-four years old, married, with two young children. He came to the United States from Bogota, Colombia, when he was twenty years old to make a better life for himself. He graduated from high school in Colombia and took several classes in college in the states without obtaining a college degree. He studied air conditioning and electrical engineering prior to becoming what he terms "a handyman." I met Diego, now an American citizen, years ago when he worked in the building where I lived in South Florida. Diego can fix most anything. He is smart and very personable, and so I asked him one day if he would give me his definition. "My definition of a successful life is to be happy and appreciative of the small and large things in life." I asked Diego what his definition of being happy was. "Happy is making a living and in the process learning something new each day as well as loving my wife and children." That was it for Diego: making a living, lifelong learning, and loving his family.

Sabrina Persaud is forty-six years old, married, with four children, and resides in New York City. She was born in Guyana, in South America, but came to America twenty-seven years ago because there were so few economic opportunities in Guyana. Sabrina has worked as a home health aide since 1998 and currently is living away from her family while taking care of a ninety-two-year-old widower who was spending the winter in Boca Raton, Florida. "My definition of a successful life," Sabrina said, "is to have a job I like to do and one that allows me to work hard. No one gave me anything. I have had to earn all I have by hard work, and I like that." I asked Sabrina to expand on her definition of a job she enjoys. "That would be a job that allows me to live a comfortable life. I am not there yet, but I hope to be someday soon. Comfortable for me means being able to live with my family and being able to give my kids a better life than the one I now have. Life doesn't give you a gold spoon. You have to work hard for a better life, and you cannot take anything for granted."

Judy Tackett is forty-seven years old and has a very demanding job as director of the Homeless Project Impact Division of Nashville Social Services. "In a successful life, we know what the goals are we are working toward. Achieving those goals becomes less important than the effort to improve, teach, share, and communicate. Goals change over time as we change with them. If goals are too static, I wonder whether we have honed in on the right purpose and whether we are truly leaving something of value behind at the end of our lives. That is, after all, what I believe defines a successful life: Leave the world a little better when we exit than it was when we entered it."

Rachael Woods, an educator and thirty-one years old, also emphasized the goal of making this world a better place in her response to the question of what constitutes a successful life. "Spreading as much good as you can and appreciating moments of peace, compassion, and warmth in the world around you."

Dr. David Spigel, a forty-seven-year-old physician who deals with life and death on a daily basis as a cancer specialist, reduced his definition to a single sentence. "For me a successful life is where I feel useful and have made a positive impact on someone else and have done more good than bad as well as having enjoyed my time."

Rabbi Shana Goldstein Mackler, age forty-one, also summed up her definition in a single sentence: "To have lived a successful life is to have experienced and shared love and laughter and labored to make a small imprint on the world for the better."

Another response involved what God expects of us and was sent to me by thirty-two-year-old Ben Grady, a database administrator at the Nashville Rescue Mission. "In my belief, a successful life is given by reflecting on the following quote from Micah 6:8: 'He has told you, O man, what is good; and what does the Lord require of you but to do justice, and to love kindness, and to walk humbly with your God.' To the extent that someone is just, kind, and walks in humble submission to God, I believe they are living a successful life."

I was intrigued by the response I received from Kim Karesh, a forty-two-year-old CEO of the Nashville Adult Literacy Council who admitted that the definition of a successful life was a question she had thought about much in her young life. She took a sabbatical to wrestle with this question in 1994 and came up with the following: "Success is a state of mind. It is not how others judge you or how they feel about your activities or your achievements. It all comes down to how you feel, not only what you do, but your motives behind your actions." She continued, "Successful people are those who do something that is helpful without causing undue harm. Success means doing the best you can with what you have, and it means acquiring new tools and resources as they become available to you so you can do better the next time. Success means holding respect for everyone you encounter, including yourself. Success is feeling calmly satisfied when you have done all of the above."

Naomi Sedek is forty years old and a leader in the Nashville Jewish Federation. She was very precise in her answer. "Live completely, love unconditionally, work passionately, and give generously. That is my definition of a successful life."

Carlos Revilledo, a forty-six-year-old interior designer, responded that to him a successful life was finding work you loved. It was a simplistic life that was filled with a balance of work and finding peace and contentment outside of work. It was not about making money but rather about finding a way to be around people to love and care about.

One day while being driven to the airport in Nashville, I had a conversation with our Lyft driver, Jeffery Hayes, age twenty-eight, who seemed to be a very thoughtful young man, and so I asked him his opinion. He responded in a clear and straightforward manner. "A successful life is one when you have made enough money to have your car paid off and able to buy a home and have enough money in the bank for a cushion for the unexpected things that happen in life." Clearly Jeffery believed that money was a link to a successful life, possibly because he had so little at the time of our ride to the airport.

I struck up a conversation during another ride to the Nashville airport one rainy morning with William Bowers, age forty-nine. William retired at age forty-five after selling his small trucking business and was driving to supplement his income as well as to have something to do during the day. William's wife was deceased, and he was raising their three children as a single parent. His initial response to my question about a successful life was similar to the success-by-proxy definition. "If my children grow up to be well-adjusted and happy with their lives, I will feel as if I had a successful life." After a few moments of reflection, however, he added, "And if I can go to sleep at night with no major regrets in my life, that, too, will be a part of my definition." Finally, as we reached the airport, he added something I have heard from most of those I interviewed: "Money is not what will bring me success."

My former assistant at work, Katita McCullough, who is forty-eight years old, had worked very hard to obtain the job she now holds. She told me one day at the office that her definition of a successful life means to have determination and to never give up when life deals you tough times. That determination will set an example for others to emulate and thus will be leaving behind something of value. "Leaving something of value behind is my definition of a successful life, and that value for me is determination."

Scott Hoffman, my forty-year-old nephew and an accomplished songwriter, award-winning musician, and founder of the pop band Scissors Sisters, had this to say: "A successful life is having a set of goals to achieve and then achieving those goals." He added that formulating these goals in life and then achieving them will not only make you successful, but it will also bring you happiness.

I spent some time interviewing Demetria Vaughn, a forty-six-year-old Nashville Metro Social Service civil servant who had two master's degrees in education and public administration. Demetria did not have to think long to answer my question. "A successful life is to be in my right mind." Not understanding what she meant by this, I asked her to explain. As a nineteen-year-old, Demetria had served in the military and was a part of Operation Desert Storm, where she witnessed real tragedy along with teamwork, camaraderie, commitment, and discipline. She also witnessed many of her comrades who were traumatized come home with PTSD and not in their right minds. She was lucky as she did not suffer any of the elements of PTSD and, therefore, believed being in your right mind was a large part of living a successful life. Along with this rather unusual definition, she added that having a strong support system and a strong faith were also elements that led to a life of success.

A nurse practitioner specializing in working with end-of-life issues for her patients, and my sister-in-law, Lucy Goldstein, age forty-three, reduced her definition to a basic response: "A successful life is one where you are grateful about small things in your life, have meaningful work, and have a life partner whom you love."

Another nurse, Teresa Wilson, age forty-eight, had this to say. "A grown, happy, healthy, and successful person who makes their mother proud fulfills the tenets of what I define as a successful life."

A third nurse, Margaret Cyr, in her forties as well, stated, "A successful life is achieving all my goals and turning around and giving it all back to help others reach their goals. Only then will I have completed God's work through me."

Angela Wilson-Liverman, forty-nine years old and director of the Vanderbilt Nurse Practitioner Division in the Department of Obstetrics and Gynecology, told me that "success is the gift of doing something you love, which is intrinsically motivating and also provides sufficient extensive motivation for you to live in a manner that provides for your basic needs and gives you peace and happiness."

Elke Hoffman, forty-two and the communication coordinator for the Vanderbilt Department of Obstetrics and Gynecology, was expansive in her response to my question. "A successful life is one that cultivates integrity, kindness, compassion, and empathy and makes a positive impact on the lives of those encountered during their time on earth. It is a life that grows from mistakes and provides others with an example of caring for the world around us, one that people can use to learn and grow from within their own set of talents." She then added that a song from the play *Wicked* said it all for her. "'Because I knew you, I have been changed for good.' That feels like success for me."

I asked one of my partners at Vanderbilt, Dr. Etoi Garrison, age forty-eight, what she thought was the definition of a successful life. "A successful life changes the course of history for someone else. A life well-lived propels the individual and those within his or her sphere of influence forward and does not just happen. It is carefully nurtured by the individual, his or her family, and faith in God." As a specialist in high-risk pregnancies, Dr. Garrison certainly changes the course of history for someone else on an almost daily basis. Her definition of a successful life clearly fits her profession.

These maturing adults defined a successful life somewhat differently than the many young individuals I had questioned. The word "happy" only appeared a very few times in their definitions, and they were fixated more on making the world a better place and a desire to make a positive difference in the lives of others. That difference need not be a large one and could be defined in different ways. Enjoying one's job or career was the second most frequently mentioned definition, followed by finding love and having a loving family and good friends as well as having dreams and goals and then achieving them. This group of twenty-five- to forty-nine-year-old individuals also mentioned once or twice: being grateful, living a moral and ethical life, being unafraid to die, having a healthy body, having a life of constant learning, being kind, never giving in to adversity, being in a right mind, having a strong faith in God, having well-adjusted children, having few major regrets, making their mother proud, and learning from their mistakes. Only three of this group put money into their definitions of a successful life.

The desire to make a positive impact on the world, as exemplified by this group, was made very clear to me when, many years ago, my mother-in-law, Dorothy Goldstein, whom I loved and admired, was diagnosed with stage 4 breast cancer. One evening at dinner, Dorothy told me how proud she was of her life's accomplishment. Feeling that she had had a successful and loving marriage, four devoted children and eight beautiful grandchildren, and hundreds of dear family members and friends, she told me that she was filled with love and pride.

Dorothy seemed to be totaling up all she had done in her life. She began listing the countless charities and organizations she had worked with, the good deeds she had accomplished, and the causes she had supported with her time and resources. Then she added that above all, she wanted to make a positive difference and now truly understood, from deep within, that indeed her life had made a positive difference. This was her final definition of what made up the elements of a successful life, and she had accomplished that goal.

These individuals in the maturing age group are living at a very exciting time of their lives. It is a time of education and finding out what it is they want to do with their lives. It is also a season of new beginnings, such as making new friends and finding relationships that are meaningful and loving. It is a time of marriage, having children, living in a community, and working to serve others in society. It is a time of learning about the rest of the world through travel and study.

Making a difference with a positive impact on other lives, the community, or even the world was the most popular definition of what makes up a successful life for this age group, just ahead of having a career and doing what you love. Americans want work they can feel good about, work that treats them fairly, and work that allows them to have a good life with family and friends. It is a mission quite different from that in many other cultures. A Chinese saying that the point of life is to work does not hold true for most Americans. Maturation brings into focus a more global view of the world and seems to lead to an emphasis on leaving the world a better place than when one entered it.

CHAPTER 4

THE MATURE

"Never lose sight of the fact that the most important yardstick of your success will be how you treat other people, your family, friends and coworkers and even strangers you meet along the way." Barbara Bush

"Never give in, never give in, never, never, never . . . never give in except to convictions of honor or good sense." Winston Churchill

"To succeed in life, one needs a good wish bone, back bone and funny bone." Reba McEntire

"Human ills come from wanting what we do not need." Maimonides

"I leave this life with no regrets. It has been a wonderful life, full and complete with the great loves and great endeavors that make it worth living. I am sad to leave but I leave with the knowledge that I lived the life that I intended." Charles Krauthammer

BETWEEN THE AGES OF FIFTY AND SEVENTY-FIVE, most of us have a very large number of experiences that teach us important lessons and make us evaluate who we are and what we want to do in the remaining years of our lives. The fifties are often called the beginning of mid-life crisis, and from there we age into the seventies as mature seniors. During this stage of life, we become individuals who, finally, are more able to evaluate how we have conducted ourselves and how well we have handled life's ups and downs.

I obtained the most definitions of what constitutes a successful life from this group, and these individuals had much to offer in helping answer the question of how individuals who have lived a relatively long time and are heading into the last chapters of life define a successful life.

Some think of fame as an ingredient to a successful life. Sixty-one-year-old Tanya Tucker has been famous since she was thirteen years old, and I wanted to learn what role being famous had played in her definition of a successful life. I have known Tanya for over thirty years, having delivered all three of her children: Presley, now thirty years old; Grayson, twenty-eight years old; and Layla, age twenty.

Tanya was born in Seminole, Texas, and at the age of thirteen recorded "Delta Dawn," a radio hit that made her a nationwide wonder. With her father, Beau, at her side, she began a career that would include a streak of top-ten and -forty hits, forty-two successful albums, and many country music awards, including Female Vocalist of the Year in 1991, and most recently two Grammy Awards for Best Country Album and Best Country Song. I went to Tanya's home in Nashville one rainy winter day in 2020 to interview this extremely talented and longtime famous country music singer.

Tanya told me that her definition of a successful life has changed often. "At first, success was just to have things, as we were poor, but not dirt poor, and then at age sixteen, I signed a multimillion-dollar contract, and, all of a sudden, I felt famous and rich. Life has had its highs and lows, and along the way, I have suffered at the hands of health problems, lack of musical hits, and the deaths of my parents. But I have survived them all and had my share of wonderful moments, such as the recent recording of my new album and very successful hit, 'Bring My Flowers Now.' That album and song brought me back from the dead."

When I asked Tanya if fame had made her feel successful, she responded that what made her feel successful was not fame but rather the birth of her three wonderful and talented children. "My children are my best awards. Fame is wonderful when you have it and not important when you don't. It makes me feel successful being able to change things that are wrong, such as helping sick children, assuring animal rights, and aiding the elderly." Tanya also told me that she wanted to make much more music as well as money, "so I can give it away for the rest of my life. I want to make a living at giving." She also mentioned, "I am grateful for the life I have lived and feel as if my life has been a successful one." Tanya smiled and quickly added, "I am a long way from being through."

My wife, Julie, and I have been friends with Crystal Gayle and her husband, Bill Gatzimos, for over thirty-two years. They have shared forty-nine wonderful years of marriage together, have two children, Catherine and Chris, and one grandchild, sixteen-year-old Elijah. Because she has known fame most of her life, I wanted to get Crystal's definition of a successful life, including how fame fit into her definition, and so I sat down in her studio in Nashville one cold February day in 2020 to interview this charming, gracious, and talented country music singer.

Crystal is sixty-nine years old. Born in Paintsville, Kentucky, Crystal was one of eight children and the only child in the family to be born in a hospital. When she was four years old, her family moved to Wabash, Indiana, where she spent her early years and where she realized that singing was what she loved to do. "Music became my life at a very young age. I sang in the church choir, my school, and anywhere else I could. My mother told me that I started singing even before I could walk."

After graduating from high school, her older sister, famous country music singer Loretta Lynn, took Crystal under her wing and introduced her to the music business. Crystal signed her first contract with Decca Records at the young age of eighteen. After she moved to United Artists Records, she became well-known for her musical hit "I'll Get Over You," but it is her 1977 release of "Don't It Make My Brown Eyes Blue" that remains her signature hit to this very day. Crystal became a star in the business, recording numerous albums and twenty-two number-one singles, as well as performing concerts throughout the world during her long, productive career.

I finally got around to asking Crystal for her definition of a successful life and whether fame was included in her definition. "My definition of a successful life is finding what you love to do and then pursuing it. Not everyone can be a singer, but I had the gift of a good voice, and I was lucky to be in the right place at the right time, had a lot of help from some very good people, and was able to do what I loved to do, which was to sing. Fame allowed me to do what I loved to do, but it does not define a successful life for me. Fame does play a role in my success, as it has given me the freedom to do so many of the things I have done in my life. But fame is just a word, and it has not led me. Being shy, I have never really thought much about fame and was often uncomfortable with all the attention I was receiving."

Crystal then told me that a successful life for her was having a loving family, which included her parents, husband, children, grandchild, and siblings, as well as enriching other people's lives. "It is nice to be recognized as someone who has enriched others by helping them through a difficult time in their lives because of my music. That makes me feel as if I have made a positive impact and is certainly one of my definitions of a successful life."

I had been hoping to interview former senator Bob Corker ever since I began writing this book. I first met Bob in 1995 when he was appointed Tennessee commissioner of finance and administration, and we worked on a task force to reform and improve Tennessee's version of Medicaid called TennCare. I had attended a talk he gave to two hundred Nashville Academy of

Medicine physicians to assure them he understood their frustrations and anger and would do all in his power to solve the many problems that existed within TennCare. In the space of just a few minutes, Bob Corker had his audience in the palm of his hand. It was a truly masterful performance, and I knew immediately that he was going to be an exceptional leader. I was not disappointed.

Born in Orangeburg, South Carolina, Bob moved to Chattanooga when he was eleven. After graduating from the University of Tennessee, he focused on the construction, development, and acquisition of real estate, operating in eighteen states across the country. In 1986, as a civic endeavor, he led the creation of Chattanooga Neighborhood Enterprise, a nonprofit organization that has to date helped more than ten thousand families secure decent and affordable housing. In 2001, five years after serving in the Tennessee government, he became mayor of the city of Chattanooga and helped transform his hometown into one of the nation's most admired cities. He was elected to the United States Senate in 2006 and was overwhelmingly re-elected in 2012. Bob was named one of the one hundred most influential people in the world by *TIME* magazine and served as the chair of the Senate's Foreign Relations Committee. During his service in the Senate, he became a national and global thoughtful leader on fiscal, financial, and foreign policy issues. Bob returned to private life in January of 2019.

Bob, sixty-eight, told me that he hoped to be productive until the last days of his life. "I worked hard after college to make something of myself, and my hard work paid off. Early in life I knew I wanted to live life in a way to do what I could to leave this world a better place for others. We all have been given special gifts, and we need to use these gifts in the most productive manner possible."

Bob told me that as mayor, he'd had a vision for his city and that achieving that vision was neither frustrating nor problematic. As commissioner of finance and administration for the state of Tennessee, he felt he could, with the flick of a pen, make good things happen for his state. However, as a United States senator, Bob noted a constant sense of wanting to do more and be more productive. "It was very different, as I had to work with so many other people to make things happen. On the other hand, the issues we dealt with were very significant." Bob managed to achieve much in his twelve years in the Senate and realized his voice was important. He was not afraid to speak out and challenge leaders of either party. "I am glad that I decided to only serve two terms in the Senate and realize that by taking that approach I was able to serve in a very independent way. I am proud of the work I did as a senator, and it was the greatest privilege of my life."

When I asked the former senator for his definition of a successful life, he had this to say: "By keeping a focus on family, friends, and community, I have tried to ensure that my business, civic, and public service efforts touched people in a positive way. I hope and believe I was successful. I want to do more using the wisdom and experiences acquired over the years in the pursuits in which I am currently involved and hope to be a part of the conversation as to where our country is going. If there is another place where I can make a difference, I would consider it, but right now I am very happy with my new life and what I am now pursuing."

I met another former United States senator, Dr. Bill Frist, in 1984 when he joined the Vanderbilt University Medical Center faculty to begin a lung and heart transplant program and joined the Medical Center's ethics committee, which I chaired. I was impressed with his interest in the work we were doing, and his input on many difficult ethical issues was very helpful. We became colleagues and friends. Bill Frist is sixty-eight years old and married and has three adult sons and nine grandchildren. He attended Princeton University and then obtained his medical degree from Harvard Medical School, following which he completed a surgical residency at Massachusetts General Hospital in Boston and a fellowship at Stanford University in California, before coming to Vanderbilt.

Bill was born and raised in Nashville and was the youngest of five children. Bill said that his father, a beloved physician and cofounder of Hospital Corporation of America, today's largest for-profit hospital chain in the United States, was a major influence in his life. Dr. Thomas F. Frist Sr. told his son that he did not need to be the wisest, but he did need to use common sense and express loyalty, friendship, and humility. He also told Bill that service to others was critical to a life well lived. Becoming a physician allowed Bill to follow much of the advice his father had given him.

During his ten years at Vanderbilt, Bill was able to help thousands of patients regain and maintain good health through the transplant service he directed. But he still wanted to do more, so with the help of many of his friends, Bill decided to run for the United States Senate. It was a thrilling time in 1994 when

Bill won the election and began a twelve-year career where he helped enact several vital and helpful pieces of legislation, such as writing the enormously popular bill in 2003 that established Medicare Advantage plans for seniors and added prescription medication coverage for all Medicare recipients. Bill later became the Majority Leader of the Senate during the presidency of George W. Bush. Bill explained that "being a physician was a vehicle to get things done for others on a one-on-one basis; however, being in government and affecting public policy allowed me to help others on a one-on-many basis." Since leaving the Senate, Bill has become a venture capitalist, using private equity to assist health companies that serve the ignored, poor, and vulnerable around the world. Bill has been on more than twenty-five global missions, worked as a surgeon in eighteen different African countries, and helped lift the lives of countless others in a meaningful and humble way.

"My definition of a successful life is a life dedicated to service. My life is 100 percent built around service to others, but that service also needs to be augmented with humility and grace. I define grace as unconditional giving. Service with humility and grace was passed down to me from my father, who I idolized and continues to influence how I act and what I do every day of my life. I feel as if my life has been and continues to be successful."

In December of 2019, I sat down with Tennessee Fifth District congressman Jim Cooper, age sixty-five, to discuss his definition of a successful life. Jim was born and raised in Middle Tennessee and comes from a political family. His father was a previous governor of Tennessee, and his brother is the current mayor of

Nashville. Jim was a Rhodes Scholar at Oxford University, graduated from Harvard School of Law, and practiced law for eleven months before being elected in 1982 as the youngest United States congressman at the time. He served in this role until 1994 when he lost an election for the Senate. Running again for Congress in 2002, Jim Cooper won and continues to serve.

Jim is a passionate advocate for an agenda that includes universal health care, a sustainable environment, more economic opportunity for all Americans, and strengthening our democracy in Tennessee. He helped raise three children, all of whom are accomplished in what they do. He also has one grandchild. "The main factor for a successful life for me is a life with reasonable expectations." While Jim Cooper expects certain things to happen, he is not surprised or necessarily upset when those things do not happen as expected. He is a realist, and this has helped him as a government leader and a person seeking a successful life. There is more, however, to his definition. A deacon in his church one Sunday uttered these words: "I got up this morning in my right mind," and these words made him realize how fortunate he has been to be able to state these same words each waking morning.

Jim has been made more aware about the importance of being in a right mind as his late wife, Martha, had been diagnosed with Alzheimer's disease. Jim continued, "The happiest people seem to march to the beat of a different drummer and do not let other people define their lives. When I was young, I wondered what I would do with my life. Coming from the family I had and meeting talented and young, goal-oriented individuals at a northeast prep school, I realized I needed to learn what it was that I really wanted to do, not necessarily what others expected of me. Becoming a lawyer and being elected to Congress, I realized this was my calling. I wanted to make a difference in the lives of others, and this was my way of doing that. I have had zero career advancement, making the same salary all my life, which is equal to what a graduate of Harvard Law School can expect to make, but money has never been a driving force for me. What does drive me is the role as mentor to hundreds of government interns over the years and to observe the incredible results of that mentoring. I am always looking for more in the work that I do in Washington, such as visible proof that America is getting stronger. All this and having a loving family helps me define my life as a successful one."

I also had the opportunity to sit down with former longtime United States congressman from Tennessee Bob Clement for a discussion on his views of what defines a life of success. Bob, seventy-five years old when we spoke, is married to a wonderful woman, Mary, and together they have two children and five grandchildren. "I knew I was going to go into public service and politics as a teenager, in part because I saw and liked that way of life from my father, who was governor of the state of Tennessee for ten years. In my lifetime, I have had seven career changes and learned that money was never going to be a driving force in my life. I have never equated money with success.

"A successful life's definition is dependent on your age. When I was young, I was very career-oriented, and by that definition, I have been successful, becoming a United States congressman and president of Cumberland College in Tennessee, much because of hard work but also learning as much from my losses as I did from my winnings. I am now, however, in another chapter in my life, which includes being a business consultant and author of a book, and so my definition has expanded. Basically, now I will feel successful if I leave this world a better place than when I entered it, and for me that would include being an effective and productive politician, a good father and grandfather, and mentor to many."

On a beautiful Nashville winter day in 2019, I went to the home of Jeff and Melinda Balser, both fifty-seven years old. Jeff was a medical student at Vanderbilt many years ago when we first met and has been elevated over the years at Vanderbilt to its highest rank of CEO of the Medical Center and dean of the Medical School. The Medical Center employs twenty-six thousand individuals, which makes Vanderbilt University Medical Center the second-largest employer in Tennessee. His wife, Melinda, currently a community volunteer and on numerous nonprofit boards, has a Vanderbilt University master's degree in divinity. Together they have three children, Jimmy, an attorney; Jillian, a social worker and therapist; and Maddie, a research assistant. Because of all their lofty accomplishments, I was eager to find out what these two highly intelligent individuals thought about the definition of a successful life.

Jeff told me his definition could be best understood by a metaphor. "How you feel when you get a gift for a holiday or special occasion is different from the more joyous feeling elicited when you give a gift to someone who is truly appreciative. Similarly, in my professional life I have also moved from positive feelings of the good things happening to me to a place where I feel even more elated when the people around me feel as if I have helped create an environment for them to succeed." Jeff believes, as the head of an extremely prestigious medical center, when he creates an environment that helps the large number of employees at Vanderbilt succeed in the work they are doing, he feels the most successful. To Jeff, creating conditions so others can grow in their professional lives defines a successful life.

Melinda had a different definition. "A successful life for me includes knowing I have raised empathetic, kind, productive, and loving children; knowing that my work is helping make the world a better place; and feeling as if I have been a sage advisor to my immediate and extended family." After listening to Melinda's definition, Jeff turned to me and said, "I echo what Melinda said about our children." These two accomplished individuals never mentioned money or fame. The only definitions that worked for them were in making a positive impact in others' lives.

I have worked for decades with Wright Pinson, sixty-seven years old and deputy CEO and chief health system officer of Vanderbilt University Medical Center. Because he is a major leader in the field of medicine and someone who has been instrumental in the incredible growth and well-being of the Medical Center, I wanted to ask for his definition of a successful life. He had fame and fortune, so what else might he have to say about success? Wright was born in New Mexico and raised in several locations as a military dependent, graduated from the University of Colorado, then obtained a master's degree in business from the University of Colorado, worked for IBM, and finally decided to go to medical school at Vanderbilt. After extensive post-medical school training, which included residency and three fellowships, Wright returned to Vanderbilt to initiate a liver transplant team.

"It was my mother who always put people at ease and who was empathetic and caring. I learned the art of medicine from watching her interact with people. I wanted to help people just as my mother did. It made sense for me to become a physician. I was so very lucky to have the parents I had. They supported and encouraged me to become educated. My definition of a successful life is one in which I have taken care of the basic needs of life as well as made significant contributions to help others."

I asked Wright to define these basic needs. "To have meaningful relationships that lift me up and support me and to be able to put a roof over my head and food on the table and have enough money to not have to struggle with many of life's burdens." While Wright admitted that his income was significant due to his role at Vanderbilt, he nonetheless spent little on himself and believed strongly that money did not bring him happiness. Wright has been in an eighteen-year loving and nurturing relationship with a woman who "lifts me up and supports me," thereby fulfilling his main definition of a successful life.

Wright also told me that one other definition of a successful life included feeling as if he had been able to help people through the travails of major illnesses and being able to support and guide patients in their quests for cures and to relieve their anxiety and suffering. He said, "Being able to help people is a great gift and allows me to feel my life is a successful one." Wright made one other important observation. "This question of a successful life is one that is usually touched upon at someone's funeral. We should attempt to answer that question for ourselves long before our funeral."

What we experience in life most certainly affects how we define a successful life, so I wanted to reach out to friends who'd endured hardship. Bobby and Brenda Rosenblum suffered the tragic loss of one of their two sons at the young age of forty-two. Brenda, age seventy and a longtime coworker with her husband in several business ventures, came right to the point when I asked for her definition. "When you lose a child you lose a part of yourself," she said. "So it is difficult for me to give you a definition of a successful life, since a significant part of me is no longer here."

Brenda dried her eyes and continued, "The part of me that remains alive, however, believes that my wonderful and loving relationships with my husband, children, grandchildren, and sisters are my crowning definition of a successful life." Bobby totally agreed that their definition of a successful life was intimately entwined in the relationships they have developed with family and friends. "It is these loving relationships that bring us happiness and define our success in life." Bobby then added, "My relationship with my spouse is the most important thing in my life." Clearly, these two thoughtful people who had suffered a great loss in their lives felt that their success's foundation was in the loving relationships they had with their family and friends. Despite their great loss, they both believe their lives have been successful.

Mary Beth Stone is a seventy-two-year-old songwriter and singer in Nashville and a member of a writing group I attend each month. She agreed to think about her definition of a successful life and send it to me. Here is what she wrote: "At one time, I would have defined a successful life simply as having a number-one hit with Carrie Underwood, Blake Shelton, or some such country megastar. As time passes and that goal remains elusive, I add to it having a life partner who will bring me soup when I'm sick and having enough money to stop having to juggle most months. But now that I am nearing the fourth quadrant of a century, what I crave most is peace, for myself and for the world. My favorite prayer, hands down, is the Jewish prayer for peace, 'Grant us peace, your most precious gift.' I have come to understand that without peace, nothing else is valuable. So, by that definition, am I successful? No, but I come closer to it all the time. I have developed a kind of Buddhist acceptance of where I am at right now, which, although sometimes difficult to summon, still cushions me and keeps me hopeful. I guess that is a kind of success."

Beverly Kirby Jones, fifty-five, became a paraplegic at the age of twenty following a tragic automobile accident. She was born and raised in Middle Tennessee, graduated from high school, married at age seventeen, and became the mother of two children prior to her life-changing event. Beverly is now divorced and lives alone. Loquacious, with a very pleasing personality, Beverly wanted to make sure I understood from the start that she was not defined by her disability. "I use a wheelchair, but I am not bound or confined to it. I am more than a person in a wheelchair."

Beverly explained that her definition of a successful life is one in which "I have had a purposeful life." I asked how she defined a purposeful life. "You start in life with a purpose and hopefully grow to understand there is meaning in everything you do. When I was injured, my mental health became important to me, and I started to think about what my purpose was. I decided that my purpose was to be able to take care of myself and my two children rather than having them take care of me. The definition of success and purpose changed as I aged. As my son and daughter grew older, my purpose expanded to educate myself, and so I chose to become a court reporter, a profession I have practiced since 1990. Later, my purpose was to take care of my elderly father, and this continues to be one of my major purposes in life to this day. Yet, there are more purposes in my life. One is to reveal to others that my way of life is not necessarily an aberration but rather just another side effect of life's ups and downs. While I am not able to walk, I am able to live a wonderful, rich, and joyful life. My being paralyzed has affected my quality of life because many things others take for granted as easy to do are difficult for me; however, I love living, and my life is a satisfying one.

"I grew up under the guidance and beliefs of the Church of Christ religion, and this has helped me understand that it is better to give than to receive. My faith has given me peace and has helped me feel that my life is exactly what it is supposed to be. God knew I could handle this obstacle, and I consider myself to be a role model. I did not choose to be physically disabled, but I hope to show others that they, too, can handle major obstacles in their lives as well." I asked Beverly if she now considers her life to be a successful one, and her answer was direct and concise. "I have taken care of myself, raised two successful children, educated myself, lived a life of faith in God, and served as a role model for many others. So, yes, I have lived a successful, meaningful, and purposeful life."

Howard Korn, a seventy-four-year-old retired dentist, is someone I have known for a relatively long time. He and his wife have a home in the same condominium as I do in South Florida. He has been happily married for fifty years and has three children and six grandchildren. Howard was raised in Brooklyn, New York, and attended New York University Dental School. Over the years, Howard and I have enjoyed occasional walks together on the beach while we talk about many of life's complex issues. Howard was diagnosed with metastatic prostate cancer over ten years ago, and I believed he would have a very interesting perspective on the definition of a successful life. Howard initially underwent surgery followed by chemotherapy a year after his surgery. I asked if he would let me interview him for my book. He agreed to my request and was quick to add, "There is not just one definition of a successful life, and there are no walls or restraints to the definition."

Howard began by saying a successful life to him was to be educated. "I am the first person in my family who graduated from college, and for me a life filled with continued education in one form or another is vital to my definition of a successful life. I had good support from my family and friends in my pursuit for an educated life, which I learned was not just about book learning but also what I could learn about life itself." Being educated, however, was not the total extent of Howard's definition of a successful life. He had one other definition that he believed was most important for him. "I believe that a successful life is being in the moment. This is how I try to live my life, and by knowing I have lived most of my life being in the moment, I feel successful. As I grew older, I was able to understand right from wrong and became able to lessen selfishness and negativity in my life. Being in the moment became more and more a part of my life, and I have gotten quite good at it, and it has been a huge help in dealing with the cancer that has been with me for so many years."

Being and living in the moment, along with being grateful and aware of life's evolving events, have contributed significantly to Howard's ability to enjoy his life even as he continues to fight his lengthy battle with cancer. That fight, however, has not dampened Howard's enthusiasm for life. He admitted that by his definition he has led a successful life.

I met Henry Lennon, a seventy-three-year-old surgeon, thirty years ago. He and his wife, Donna, became good friends with my wife, Julie, and me, sharing many life events together over the years. Henry was born in a displaced persons camp in Nuremberg, Germany, with his parents being survivors of Auschwitz, Bergen-Belsen, and Dachau concentration camps. He and his family immigrated to Australia, where he was raised and lived until he moved to the United States, married, began a practice of maxillofacial surgery, and raised his two daughters in Boca Raton, Florida.

Henry was diagnosed in February 2019 with stage 4 pancreatic cancer, and the statistics weighed heavily against his survival. He was shocked with this sudden and unexpected diagnosis but told me that he had no intention of dying and would do everything in his power to survive, which so far has included many rounds of chemotherapy and surgery. Since Henry was literally fighting for his life, I asked him one day as we sat in the living room of his home if he would consider giving me his definition of a successful life. He graciously agreed, stating that he found this existential exercise to be very cathartic for him.

"I used to think that he who dies with the most toys wins the title of 'Mr. Success.' Nothing could be further from the truth. Money and possessions mean nothing when you do not have your health. Life becomes merely an existence if you do not have support and love from your family and friends. I am blessed to have a wonderful support group headed by my wife, my daughters, and my beautiful granddaughter, as well as my wonderful friends. Yes, I have achieved success in my professional life and have had more than I had ever dreamed was possible. But now that I feel deeply that my mortality is at stake, all superficial successes mean naught. I struggle each day to maintain my sanity and health, but when I eventually succumb to my disease, my life will have been defined by those whom I love and cherish, and that is the definition I choose for success."

Fifty years old, Yvonka Lyons, an administrative assistant in a physician's office, told me that her definition of a successful life was quite simple. "Being able to accept yourself for who you are and no longer looking for validation from other people."

Joe Freedman, fifty-two and a self-pronounced serial entrepreneur, had this to say. "I would define a successful life as one that is lived with few regrets and never spending time on

Someday Isle. When I am on my deathbed, I will know I lived a successful life if each year I was a better husband, father, friend, and mentor than I was the previous year."

Jennifer Stanton, a fifty-one-year-old nurse, told me, "A successful life is a life lived where one's most valuable possessions cannot be measured or even held in one's hands."

A medical scientist at Vanderbilt, Dr. Kaylon Tran, age fifty-three, responded to my question with a single sentence that also embodies a retrospective view. "If at the end of my life, I can honestly say that the world is better off because I was here, then for me that will be a successful life."

Fifty-year-old Kathy Carlson, a newspaper editor in Nashville, had this to say: "A successful life is one when you have spent a life treating other people kindly, finding and doing work that you love and that helps make the world a better place, finding and contributing to a community in which you and others can thrive and continue learning new things throughout life, and appreciating the beauty that the world has to offer." Kathy had listed several important criteria to a successful life, many of which I heard repeated often.

Michael Rosen, age fifty-three and cofounder of Provider Trust in Nashville, also wrote a short but to-the-point definition. "A successful life is a love for and of life. This embodies respect for others, putting someone else first, and sharing the great things life can offer when your heart is open."

Senior computer technician at Vanderbilt University Medical Center Tom Daniel is fifty-four years old and married with a ten-year-old son. He was tested in the genius range as a young man and is considered an incredible expert in the field of computer technology. I sat down with him one afternoon at my home, where he had come to help me with a computer problem. "A successful life to me is first of all to have no significant regrets, and second that my son will grow up to have more than I have and that he will be successful in his own way." Tom went on to say that he was a relatively happy guy with a good job, and that while he could make more money elsewhere, he needed the security the job at Vanderbilt gives him, especially in that it will help finance his son's college education. "My son means so very much to me, and his success will be mine as well." Tom had used the definition of successful life by proxy.

Dr. Scott Pearson, a fifty-four-year-old professor of surgery at Vanderbilt University Medical Center, sent me his definition of a successful life. "If I have provided for the ones I love, been a comforter to others along their path, stood as steward on my bit of ground, and passed as acceptable in the eyes of my creator, then I will consider my life to be successful."

Giovanni Archoe, also fifty-four, is a program manager at the Metro Social Services in Nashville with BA and MS degrees. Divorced with no children, she told me, "A successful life constitutes having a close and loving family who display unconditional love and respect as well as long-standing, close, and nurturing friends. But it also includes attaining the goals I had set for myself, which included obtaining a good education and a job that I truly love." Giovanni is an only child who says that her friends are now her family, which helps explain why her definition of a successful life emphasizes having close and nurturing friends. She also had a very loving family with wonderful role models in her mother and grandmother. This also explains why having a close family that displays unconditional love is part of her definition.

Bonnie Campbell, a college-educated fifty-five-year-old administrative assistant in Nashville government, added, "A successful life is having a loving family and a strong faith in God, having a job you enjoy, and being able to go home each day knowing that you are able to pay the bills and have a little savings, and overall being able to enjoy life."

Not everyone felt they had yet accomplished what they needed in order to achieve a successful life. Chris Simonsen is a fifty-five-year-old real estate agent and part-time actor and singer. "My definition is certainly not financially driven. It is basically that I want to make a positive impact on my community, which includes my family, friends, and everyone I interact with in my day-to-day life. Unfortunately, because I am hard and critical on myself, I do not believe I have yet reached the level of success that for me defines a successful life. I will need to sell more homes, act in more plays, sing more songs, and perhaps then my critical nature will stabilize or perhaps be reduced, and when that time comes in my life, I might then feel as if my life has been successful." Chris's cautious nature was on display when he added, "I may never reach that level, but I hope to one day."

I had a most interesting discussion regarding the definition of a successful life with Abdelghani Barre, a social analyst working for the Nashville Metro Social Services. He was born in Somali, Africa, but came to America in 1989 and later earned his American citizenship. He graduated from Vanderbilt University where he obtained a master's degree in economics. Barre is fifty-eight years old and married with two children, ages seventeen and twenty. A devout Muslim, he's a former president of the Islamic Center of Nashville. He has been a friend of mine for over ten years.

In response to my question, Barre began by telling me that when he was a young boy, he knew he did not want to live in his father's shadow. His father was a very wealthy man in Somali and had a prominent name and reputation. Barre told his father when he was in college that he wanted to go to another land where nobody knew who he was. He wanted to be accepted and appreciated for who he was and not for where he came from. As he told his father, "I want to be sure that whatever I achieve is because of me and not you." He loved his father and had a good relationship with him; yet, for him to find success, he needed to do it on his own without his father's influence. In that sense, Abdelghani said to me, "Becoming a man of my own made me successful." He added, "Becoming educated, moving to another land, getting out of debt, providing for my family, and having friends are the ingredients that have produced a successful life for me. But the best thing of all is that I did it my way."

Jodie Barringer is a fifty-four-year-old real estate agent and neighbor of mine. Jodie is divorced and the mother of two girls in their early twenties. "A successful life for me will be in knowing that my kids will live an ethical and moral life." She was echoing the definition of success by proxy. I asked her to expand on this definition. "Life comes full circle as we move from youth to old age. We start with few material items when we are young and then accumulate so much more as we grow older. Later in our lives, when we move into nursing homes or begin to downsize our lives, we take very little with us, resembling what we had when we were young. I take from this the idea that what we accumulate material-wise in life is truly unimportant, as we wind up with so little when we near the ends of our lives. Because of this, it is important that I pay attention to the things in life that truly count, such as living an ethical and moral life. That is what I want from myself and for my children. That is success to me."

Fifty-eight and single with no children, Meryl Strassner, a New York lawyer specializing in conflict resolution, was emblematic of the premise that personal lifestyles and experiences lead to a variety of definitions of a successful life. "Being successful includes creating and then enjoying experiences that allow for many wonderful memories, which then allows for good feelings and contentment. I have practiced law, traveled, gone scuba diving, visited many museums, theaters, and other artistic events, and all these have given me the many memories that make me feel content and successful."

Josh Silva, a fifty-four-year-old security officer from Brazil, was straightforward in his response to my question. "A successful life is to be able to follow your dreams and to do what you want to do in life. I am not there yet but hope to be someday."

Amy Martin, fifty-five years old and previously an office manager of a high-rise condominium in South Florida, told me that a successful life "is being happy with yourself." I asked her how she defined happiness. "Happiness means being content with who you are and with the life you are living. It also involves not allowing things to get you down."

An experienced nurse, Toni Donegan, fifty-six, with whom I had worked for decades, was willing to let me know her thoughts on what constituted a successful life. "To me a successful life is having someone to love and to be loved by. That would include my precious husband, children, family, and friends. It also includes having good health, a safe haven in the storms of life, and a personal relationship with Jesus, who makes my life complete. It does not include a perfect life, but that looking back I can say it has been generally a good life and one that has been blessed during both the darkest and sweetest of times."

Gail Biro, fifty-seven years old and a director of organizational performance in Nashville, told me that her definition of a successful life "is to have all the things money cannot buy, such as family, friends, and health, and to have the resources to enjoy them to the fullest."

Dr. Steve Staggs, age fifty-seven and a former student of mine, had this to say: "To find true love; to find a task or job that you truly enjoy or love; to realize the gratitude of just being in a relationship with God, family, and friends."

I met with Nedeljko Zivak, a fifty-eight-year-old refugee from Bosnia and an employee of The Temple in Nashville. Nedeljko came to America in 1997 and is married with two children with college graduate degrees. He came to America for a job and a better life, both of which he has achieved, and he became an American citizen ten years ago. "A successful life to me is the one I have right now. I have a good job. My wife has a good job. My kids are college graduates. I have enough money to live the life I wish to live. I am so very happy now. I have the respect of those I work with, and I am so very happy. I am living a successful life." This was an uncomplicated man whose goals were dictated by his former life in another country and who now had achieved everything he had hoped to achieve.

One beautiful fall day in Nashville I decided to stop by my local fire station. I met Walter Luna immediately upon entering the station, and he agreed to be interviewed. Walter is fifty-eight years old and has been a firefighter for the past thirty-one years and is married with two children. He said he'd wanted to be a fireman since he was a boy. Being a fireman has given him financial security, benefits, and an exciting and adventurous job. Firemen witness their share of tragedy and heartache on a daily basis, so I wanted to assess how a life dedicated to saving lives as a fireman might have affected his definition. Walter came right to the point.

"My definition is defined in three categories: Christ, family, and job." I asked him if would explain each of these areas. Walter told me that Christ is first because he was raised as a Christian, and each time in his life when he strayed from the path of Christ, life dealt him problems, but when he changed his ways and followed Christ's teachings, his life became calm and peaceful. "Having a loving family includes my parents, wife, and children. You can't teach your kids what you don't know, so part of my success is teaching my children the way of Christ. Finally, my job makes me feel good about myself, as I am helping people in need." I asked Walter if he had saved any lives, and he responded with a soft and humble "yes." I told him of the

Jewish saying that "anyone who saves one life saves all human-ity." He smiled and told me he liked that. Walter then added, "If I can feel good about these three parts of my definition, I will feel happy and successful." I was not surprised that Walter was a pious man. His faith helps and guides him as he performs a job often filled with life's tragedies.

I interviewed Norma Fair, a fifty-nine-year-old administra-tive assistant at the Vanderbilt University Medical Center who is married with two children ages twenty-seven and thirty-four. "A successful life to me is to know that both of my children are successful. My son is a captain in the air force, and my daugh-ter is a biology teacher in Nashville, married with one child. I feel that my children are successful, so I feel as if I have been successful." Norma was not finished: "As part of my definition, I need to add having a strong faith in God, being in a loving relationship with my husband, and being financially stable. In all these regards, I believe I have lived a successful life."

One of my partners at VUMC, Dr. Ted Anderson, age sixty, a nationally known expert in minimally invasive surgery and current president of the prestigious American College of Obstetricians and Gynecologists, sat down with me one day to give his definition. "Success is having something to do every day that you find fulfilling, having someone with whom to share the good and bad in your life, and leaving a legacy by making some type of a contribution for the next generation to use in a productive manner."

The chairman of the Department of Obstetrics and Gynecology at Vanderbilt, Dr. Ronnie Alvarez, age sixty, believes,

"A successful life is one in which you worked hard, were nice to people, and stayed true to yourself yet were willing to take risks and get out of your comfort zones as well as able to look back and know that you had enjoyed the journey."

Nina Pacent is sixty years old and an editorial and music writer who I recently met when attending a Saturday morning Torah study class at The Temple in Nashville. She sent me the following definition of a successful life: "I think when people are asked what constitutes a successful life, they have a different measure of success for other people than they do for themselves. I have a friend who has many times told me that she hasn't contributed to the community in any meaningful way and that her job as an antique dealer isn't helping anybody. Yet when one of my other friends suffered the unexpected death of a former partner and was overwhelmed with details in settling the estate, my friend, the antique dealer, went over, assessed some of the items, and gave free advice on how to proceed in the estate sale. She repeated the process when another friend of mine needed to move her mother into a nursing home and money was of extreme concern. My friend, the antique dealer, went over, surveyed some of the woman's belongings, and again gave free advice to help avoid costly errors in selling the items. When I pointed out to the antique dealer how much she had helped others at a stressful time with her unique knowledge and experience, I became aware of how anybody in any profession can help others in need, changing their circumstances and, in turn, living a successful life."

Responding by email to my question of what defines a successful life, Jode Freyholtz-London, sixty years old, divorced and a mother of four, was quite specific. "I can tell you it isn't money or at least tons of it. Success is finding something you love to do so much you would do it for free and then getting good enough at it that someone is willing to pay you. I am at a place where living in a tin shed near Nimrod, Minnesota, population sixty-nine, surrounded by pines and sand, is success. No mortgage, no credit card debt, no car payment, and a more than full-time job with a mission I care about . . . mental health."

Harriet Greenberg, a sixty-one-year-old accountant in New York City, wife, and mother of two sons, told me that "a successful life is one in which you are happy with what you have, which for me means feeling satisfaction in my work and in my relationship with family and friends." Having heard this several times before, I asked her to expand on that comment, and so she added, "Happiness is attitude-driven, while success is goal-driven. A state of happiness is more than euphoric episodes; it is making the best of the life we have."

Emma Harris is a sixty-one-year-old hairdresser who has cut my hair for the past forty years. She said, "A successful life is one in which you have made an impact on other lives in a positive way and that others have also made a positive effect in your life. All we have in life are our family and friends, and so a successful life is also one in which you leave memories that your family and friends find comforting and enriching."

I asked my sister-in-law, Gretchen Goldstein, to share her definition. Gretchen, sixty-two and a civic volunteer, had much to say. "A successful life to me is one in which I have loved deeply and fully and was loved in return. Money will not make you happy or necessarily successful. Success includes for my children to be good citizens of the world and to enjoy the simple joys of everyday life. It also includes giving back more than you take from this world in kindness, service, and love, and making the world a better place." Gretchen concluded after a moment of reflection, "To be able to know that I wake up each day with gratitude in my heart for all life's blessings; to know that through my actions and deeds I have found purpose and meaning and have had a positive impact on the lives of my family, friends, and others."

Her husband and my brother-in-law, Randy, a sixty-three-year-old financial advisor, expressed his definition of a successful life. "A successful life is one in which I have raised a family comprised of children who shared my values. It includes having close friends, having a good reputation in my community, leaving behind something I can be proud of, and finally, sharing my resources with those in need."

Bruce Zeitlin, sixty-one, a home builder, felt my question was unanswerable because it was constantly evolving. However, with that caveat, Bruce added, "One has lived or is living a successful life when one can experience life through one's heart instead of one's mind, when one has realized the answer to the question 'am I my brother's keeper?' is yes, and when one wants what one has."

Julie Smith, sixty-one, the assistant to the Obstetrics and Gynecology Department chair at Vanderbilt University Medical Center, is married and the mother of four children. She told me that a successful life for her was living a balanced life. "That means there is a healthy balance between my faith, my family, and my work." Julie stressed it was her strong faith in God that helped sustain her and her family through life's ups and downs. "My husband is my best friend, and my children are my legacy, and my work gives me a feeling of accomplishment and self-worth." Julie emphasized that paying equal attention to these three aspects of her life was the balance she sought in her quest to live a successful life.

Julius Witherspoon, age sixty-two and employed by the Metro Social Service as a planning analyst for the past eight years, agreed to be interviewed for my question. Julius obtained a bachelor's and master's degree from Tennessee State University and is married with one son. Julius told me that a successful life entails faith and family and that it is the pursuit of happiness that constitutes success. "It is not necessarily achieving happiness," he said, "but it is the pursuit that truly counts." He added that success in his faith is defined as living a Christian life, and success in his family life is reached if his family was proud of him, respected him, and could depend on him.

These two issues of faith and family have not been easy ones for Julius to conquer. "There are people who are without hope or who are only looking for a free meal or voucher. There are many who I see who have stopped dreaming. They are just surviving day to day. If a person becomes poor in spirit and has lost all hope, that, to me, is the definition of an unsuccessful life. I was homeless for twenty months at age twenty-six to twenty-eight, and I lived with my sister and I was depressed and had poor spirit. My mother's words, 'You are better than this,' turned me around and helped me through this most difficult time and to a life I now consider successful."

Carolyn Naifeh, age sixty-two, cofounder and executive director of Our Place, sent a short answer in response to my question. "I believe a successful life is one in which you've loved others and been loved and also been able to work for the good of others and touch their lives in a positive way."

Betty Cortner is sixty-two years old and an administrative officer at VUMC. She's someone I have worked with for several decades. When I asked for her definition, she asked if she could think about it and email me. Betty responded several days later. "Being able to hold on to your faith through your lifetime definitely contributes to a successful life for me. Success comes from the heart. I have two beautiful girls and five wonderful grandchildren, so I have success. Success is also loving your job and the people you work closest with, and so in this regard, I am also successful. While I do not have everything I wanted in life, I have a strong faith, a loving family, and a job I love doing. I believe my life is a successful one."

Sandra Scruggs is sixty-three years old, married with three children and four grandchildren, and has worked as a seamstress and housekeeper for the past thirty-five years. Sandra told me that her definition of a successful life was first "to figure out what you want to do with your life, stick with that plan, and don't give up even if you fail from time to time. When I was young, I set my goals to be a model and a dress designer. Unfortunately, I got sidetracked with marriage and children and had to let the goal of becoming a model go. However, I was able to work as a seamstress and dress designer for many years. When the store I worked for closed, I once again was sidetracked and began working as a housekeeper, although I still do dress designing and seamstress work for several clients. Despite not totally living up to my definition of a successful life, I came as close as possible to achieving some of my dreams and goals." Sandra concluded with the comment, "I have had so very many responsibilities in my life as a wife, mother, grandmother, and provider, and while some of my dreams and goals were not reached, all in all I feel that my life has been a successful one."

Jan Ricklin, a sixty-three-year-old former president of a men's wholesale business and married with no children, sat with me one day in South Florida. She told me that finding love and having enough money to live whatever dream you may have were the basic components of living a successful life. She hesitated for a moment and then added on a personal note that success in business did not define a successful life for her, but rather finding love late in life was the ultimate dream for her, and now that she has found that love, she feels her life to be successful.

Jacqueline Hutton, sixty-three, is a community volunteer and activist in Nashville. Married with no children, Jax, as she is known by her friends, told me her definition is one in which she has reached a balance between personal achievement, close loving relations, and community involvement. Personal achievement involved taking care of her body and mind as well as being able to love herself. The loving relationship she shares with her husband and a few very close friends is what constitutes her second aspect of a successful life, and the community involvement includes working to help others in need on the street where she lives as well as those throughout the world. "While I have not always been in balance with these three elements of a successful life, I am currently in a healthy balance, and I feel successful."

Jax's husband, Robert Hutton, is sixty-nine years old and a physician specializing in emergency medicine. He told me that his definition of a successful life was one in which he has remained honest in all his dealings with family, friends, and patients, and it also includes knowing that he has taken good care of those who needed him. "I believe I have done my share in helping the world become a better place by caring for the sick and taking care of anyone regardless of their ability to pay." Robert added, "Success for me entails knowing that I have been there for those I love and who love me. My job is to place others in need ahead of myself." Asked if he has reached a place of a successful life, Robert smiled and uttered, "Absolutely."

I interviewed a very close friend, Ellen Dansky, who is sixty-five years old and a speech therapist. "A successful life is one in which you feel good about yourself, having no significant regrets and having learned from what mistakes you do make. It also includes having a job I love and being able to give back something of value to my friends, family, and community. But wait, there is more. Being grateful with what I have and being content and at peace with who I am. And one more thing: all the money in the world without these basic elements will not result in a successful life."

A sixty-five-year-old nurse at VUMC, Terrell Smith, had this to say about her definition of a successful life. "Knowing in my heart that I have made a difference in someone's life is the main element of a successful life, and for me that means that I have helped the homeless, welcomed the stranger in my home, cared for the sick, held someone who was frightened, encouraged those without help, provided for children to attend school who would otherwise never have been able to attend, and made someone laugh." She then added, "If people smile when they think of me and tell a story of how I once helped them, and if I can fulfill Psalm 100's command to 'Serve the Lord with gladness,' then I will have lived a successful life."

A sixty-five-year-old lawyer and active member of our Jewish Temple in Nashville, Martin Sir told me that each morning while doing yoga, he recites a prayer that reminds him to love God with all his heart, soul, and strength. "I believe the God we are commanded to love cannot be completely defined by humans, but I do believe God's essence includes all humanity, since we were created in God's image. So, when I can love myself and the people I encounter each day, I am loving God. A successful life to me then is when I am able to live out the words of the morning prayer that commands me to practice lovingkindness for myself and others."

The wife of a rabbi, Patricia Davis, age sixty-five, responded to my question with a self-reflective nuance. "To me a successful life is being able to look oneself in the mirror with full knowledge that one has done the right thing, is honest with oneself and secure in one's relationships, and has done the best for family and friends as well as those less fortunate."

Also age sixty-five, Shirley Speyer was succinct and specific. "A successful life is all about family, friends, and faith. To have a loving family, close and trusting friends, and a strong faith in God are the bedrock of a successful life." For Shirley, that was enough.

Joyce Hillman, a very calm and peaceful person with a beautiful smile and demeanor, is a sixty-five-year-old planning analyst for the Metro Social Services of Nashville and married with three sons, all of whom she described as employed and successful. She attended Tennessee State University and received a master's degree in social work from the University of Tennessee. Joyce told me that her definition of a successful life is when you feel you are true to your beliefs, which includes spiritual as well as relational, which she described as how you view other people. If you have done things for others because of your moral values and not necessarily what is expected of you, then that is her definition of a successful life. She went on to say, "I want to go to sleep at night knowing that I have done and am doing the right thing for myself and especially for others. My entire belief system brings me comfort."

Stewart Perlman, a sixty-five-year-old retired anesthesiologist, was more expansive in his definition. He stated his definition as follows:

1) "Loving and enjoying my Judaism and taking part in keeping it alive, which would include taking an active part in my temple as well as the Jewish Federation in the city I live.

2) Having a partner in life and sharing our love together.

3) Raising children and seeing them grow into adults, continuing to make all efforts to remain close to them, and sharing in the joy of their children, my grandchildren.

4) Enjoying life each day, remembering that God gives us great things during our lives as well as bumps in the road. We should remember to cherish the good things in life, celebrating each one of them, and to use our friends and family to guide us through the rough and difficult times in our lives.

5) Giving to charities in all things I believe in, such as the State of Israel, my temple, and the preservation of all God's creatures, such as dogs, elephants, dolphins, gorillas, and whales.

6) My success should include being happy often, smiling, laughing, and having as many cherished friendships as possible.

7) Taking care of the wonderful body and mind that God gave me by eating healthily and exercising regularly as well as practicing both yoga and meditation.

8) In addition to all this, to live a successful life, I should be involved in lifelong learning."

I heard from several individuals that a strong faith was important to the evolution of a successful life, and so I reached out to several men who join me at a monthly Evangelical Christian men's discussion group to hear what they had to say about this aspect of success. Dave Oh, fifty years old, sent me the following: "A successful life is one where I can teach my daughter about God's strength and his wondrous works so that she can pass them to the next generations and all the generations to come."

Michael Sheppard, seventy-four, responded, "Success in this life is experiencing joy by first knowing the talents you have, then exercising those talents to benefit others and, most importantly, giving God the glory."

Leoncia Dominguez, age fifty, wrote, "A successful life is a life of forgiveness and honor. When I have experienced a very personal forgiveness in my heart toward others, I have felt the most energized than at any other moment in my life. I feel the most powerful when I honor my loved ones; forgiving them is my path to success."

Bill Smith, a sixty-six-year-old employee of the Second Harvest Food Bank in Nashville, also responded by email. He wrote, "I measure success against my purpose in life. That purpose flows from the Judeo-Christian version of God and from three types of purpose. 1) There is a general purpose for mankind, which includes praising God. I succeed in that purpose both in the way I conduct my life and in intentional acts of worship. 2) There is an ongoing purpose for which God made me. Fulfilling that purpose, in my case as a writer, is a continual joy in both paid and volunteer employment writing grant proposals, promotional material, stories, and speeches and in editing people's work. Perhaps it can be said that joy in the doing is as much a measure of success as the outcome of the doing. 3) There are the temporary purposes in life that also help in defining a successful life. For me these temporary purposes included relief work for refugees streaming out of Eastern Europe in 1988 and helping my wife start a nonprofit organization that now annually cares for two hundred victims of human trafficking." Bill ended his email by stating, "I believe everyone has a purpose appointed by God. If we discover and keep focused on these three purposes, then our lives can be considered successful."

Marty Israel, sixty-seven years old and a former option trader on Wall Street, had this to say: "Being happy with the job that you have chosen, being able to give to others, and living a spiritual life are the basic elements of a successful life."

Mark Freedman, sixty-six, now retired from his role as executive director of the Jewish Federation of Nashville and Middle Tennessee, injected his usual good sense of humor into his definition: "A successful life is 1) not having a good answer to the question, 'If you had to do it all over again . . .' ; 2) having so many pleasant memories that you hardly know which one to think about first; and 3) ultimately, being in the VIP line at Heaven's Pearly Gates."

Loretta Saff is a neighbor and friend and someone who also joins me in a monthly writers group session where we share some of our written works with each other. Loretta is a Certified Life/Transition/Retirement Coach and is married to a mathematics professor at Vanderbilt. She has three daughters and six grandchildren. I asked Loretta if she would give me her definition of a successful life, and this is her response: "I believe that the foundation for success along the curvy and often rocky road of life is to have a positive mental outlook. When people become more self-aware and choose to be more positive, life becomes more enjoyable. They become kinder, hold fewer grudges, and certainly are a lot more fun to be around. This self-awareness and choosing to be positive also builds resilience, increases clarity, boosts confidence, and results in a renewed sense of optimism. I believe that having a positive mental outlook allows for a much smoother road to 'Happily Ever After' and is my definition of a successful life."

I spent one beautiful afternoon at the home of a friend I have known for many years to obtain his definition of a successful life. Bernie Pargh, an entrepreneur, is sixty-eight years old, married, with two grown children. Bernie started his career after graduating from the University of Tampa by selling electronic equipment from the back of his car. Establishing a national catalog wholesale distributing company, he built this company to a point where he was able to sell it in 1978 at the age of twenty-seven. Bernie's definition of a successful life is to leave this world a better place than when he entered it. "That's it," he exclaimed when I asked him if there was more to this definition. Bernie has clearly made this world better in many ways through his philanthropy and presently has focused his energy and resources to the refinement of the Nashville Temple cemetery.

I asked him what it was about the cemetery that aroused such a passionate interest. "In Jewish tradition, we are told that even before a house of worship is built, there needs to be an available cemetery. The cemetery is a place where no one will thank you for the work you do in establishing and maintaining this place of eternal rest, and I feel good about doing something for people who can never say thank you. It makes me feel good about myself and my life." Bernie told me that he subscribed to the saying that to those to whom much has been given, much is expected. Being somewhat of a character, Bernie also especially liked the saying by George Bernard Shaw that has become his life's philosophy: "A reasonable man adapts himself to the world around him, while the unreasonable man expects the world to adapt to him. Therefore, all progress is made by unreasonable men." He ended our time together saying, "I have worked and played hard, and I have been very lucky in my marriage and my family, and because of all this I believe I have lived a successful life."

Steve Greil, sixty-eight years old and retired after thirty years in the entertainment industry, is a member of a men's discussion group we both attend at The Temple in Nashville. His definition of a successful life included "feeling good about life and satisfied with my career; having the support of important relationships with family and friends; letting go of any angst over my past mistakes, regrets, and failures; being independent and responsible throughout my life; having pride in my role in the community I live in; knowing that I have made a difference in my community; and loving and feeling loved by many people with whom I have been able to maintain and deepen our relationships."

A good friend who is sixty-eight years old and a successful entrepreneur in Nashville sent me his definition of a successful life; however, he wanted to remain anonymous. His definition of a successful life relates to living by the following code of conduct: "1) Every day, find ways to show how much I love and value those around me. 2) Respect others by being compassionate even when I may not understand entirely. 3) Listen with compassion and without judgment and discover the true meaning behind the words of others, and speak honestly. 4) Ask about others' feelings and try to understand others' wants, needs, feelings, anxieties, and the meaning of their words. 5) Respect and honor family. 6) Find ways to contribute to a better world. 7) Be determined and tenacious about tending to all my relationships and all my pursuits. 8) Help others and be dependable. If I can live by these codes of conduct, I will have had a successful life."

Charles Krivcher, age sixty-eight, wanted to think about my question and decided to write his thoughts down rather than to give them to me orally. Charles is a lawyer and a retired soldier who served twenty years as an intelligence officer in the United States Army reserve, retiring at the rank of lieutenant colonel. To Charles, a successful life is defined as one in which a good faith effort is made to adopt as much of the Boy Scouts of America creed as possible. These attributes include being trustworthy, loyal, helpful, friendly, courteous, kind, obedient, cheerful, thrifty, brave, clean, and reverent. He wanted to also add items such as appreciation for justice, mercy, charity, and equality of the unalienable rights to life, liberty, and the pursuit of happiness to his definition. Charles stressed that above all else, "treating others as we want to be treated" is the basic foundation of living a successful life.

Dean Rothschild, age sixty-eight, is the founder and owner of a successful, large insurance company in Munster, Indiana, and a close friend. It was important for him that I know that money, while important in life, was not a determining factor in his definition of what makes up a successful life. Rather, he emphasized that closeness of family and friends are the biggest components of his definition. He also added, "If I lie down at night and feel contentment in my heart with no remorse, this contributes to my definition." His wife, Janine, also weighed in on my question. "Successful, for me, means a happy life. My family is what makes me happy, as does volunteering and caring for others."

Randy Rayburn, sixty-nine years old, is a very successful restaurateur in Nashville. He responded with his definition of a successful life as follows: "Few regrets, happy children, good business, honorable reputation, knowing and true to one's self, peace with my higher power."

Ray Pasquin, a resident of South Florida and a sixty-eight-year-old professional comedian, had a list of what he defined as a successful life: 1) Having a strong faith, 2) having a good sense of humor and being able to laugh at yourself and at life around you, 3) having the ability to accept others for who they are and being able to forgive others for what they have done, 4) making family come first and feeling as if you did your best to help your family through life's ups and downs, and 5) having a job or career you enjoy and respecting others in what they do.

Sixty-six years old and a retired auto mechanic now employed at a condominium security desk in Boca Raton, Florida, Armen Melkonian defined a successful life as one in which you work hard at something you enjoy, then added that a good family life is crucial to a successful life. "If you are honest in all your dealings with your family, friends, and others, you are successful."

Denise Alper, a sixty-one-year-old civic volunteer and self-proclaimed "perpetual student" had this to say about her definition. "A successful life is finding peace in one's life, which entails the absence of conflict with family and friends.

This means being able to rise above things that are petty and to ignore insecurities and negative memories. Most important is the relationship I have with my children. If that is a good one, then I have been successful. Success also means being able to feel as if I have been creative, tasted adventure, minimized regret, and lived a life of which my late father would have been proud."

Another close friend for many years, Kerry Brock, sixty-one, an artist, former TV personality, wife, and mother, responded, "A successful life is beating back family demons that enter your life and not letting those demons become your fears. It is also learning to love and have empathy as well as having the knowledge that nothing is about just you but rather is about something grander. It is achieving real connections with others in your life. Being less involved with self and more involved with others will make you feel more successful." Here again we can witness a definition carved out of events occurring in early life.

A cousin by marriage, Renee Alterman is someone I have known for decades, so I asked her how she would define a successful life. Renee, sixty-eight years old, is a divorced mother with three children and three grandchildren. She is retired and lives alone. "Being happy with what I have and having enough money to occasionally be able to spend time by the ocean and appreciating the small pleasures that life offers would best define my criteria of a successful life." She and I talked about my generic definition of a successful life, and she added, "Despite the downs that life has dealt me, I am nonetheless grateful for what I have and for being able to have overcome the negative genetic and environmental influences in my life."

Mitzie Russell, a sixty-three-year-old executive assistant to the clergy at The Temple in Nashville is married, has raised three children, and has eight grandchildren and three great-grandchildren. Her definition of a successful life involved success by proxy. "My measures of success are my children. If they are successful and happy with themselves, with an internal sense of contentment with the choices they have made, then I feel successful." Mitzie then added, "The measure of my success is the same as the one I have for my children. Success is not defined in monetary terms or by being at the top of a ladder. Whatever rung of the ladder you are on, if you are content being on that rung, you are successful."

Janet Hobson, a sixty-six-year-old director of Metro Government State Trial Court, emailed me her response. "My idea of a successful life is living with purpose and being passionate about doing what God created you to accomplish on earth. Living out your purpose with a grateful heart will make for an overall happy attitude and successful life. I believe that when you are truly living and doing what God has called you to do, he will supply all your material needs and give you more than you ever expected. You are then placed in a position to give back to others who are less fortunate, who need a hand up and not a handout. The people I run into who are always smiling and really appear to be enjoying life will tell you that they are just grateful and thankful that they were blessed to be living a life of purpose."

Mike Franklin, a sixty-one-year-old fire service man, stated that a successful life can be ongoing to the very end. He then listed several items in his definition. "Regardless of your position or status in life, realizing the wonder of the small things in life such as taking a nap, going to a movie or a reunion, or taking a trip helps every day in fulfilling the definition of a successful life. Also, having contemporaries in life who value your opinions and input, as well as being able to overcome one's fears in life." Mike concluded with a final definition: "Having some sense of contentment with the reputation that you have established for your epitaph."

Dr. Charles A. Levin, a sixty-one-year-old member of the Department of Psychology at Baldwin Wallace University, wrote me with a singular definition. "When I get to the end of my life, I hope I can say that I have left the world a better place than I found it."

Vickie Lawson, a sixty-three-year-old Tennessee social worker, currently the director of adult protective services for the state, wrote me, "What defines a successful life is the ability to serve God, the ability to serve others, and the ability to see humor in most every situation."

Floyd Shechter is sixty-five and president of Smart Space, a company he founded that leases and manages office space. Floyd is a successful businessman as well as a thoughtful and introspective individual whom I have worked with and known for many years. Floyd based his definition on two quotes by the journalist Hunter S. Thompson, who wrote, "Life is indeed a journey. Who is more successful, the one who experiences the storm of life or the one who has stayed safely onshore? The journey of life from cradle to grave should be lived each day with intention. When the journey comes to a close, one who lives a successful life is able to look back and proclaim, Wow! What a ride!" Floyd answered the question by asking a thoughtful and quite basic question. "When it is over, will I be able to say 'wow'?"

On March 5, 2018, I received an email from Dr. Larry Pass in response to my request for his definition of a successful life. Larry, a gifted thoracic surgeon and a dedicated family man, wanted to take Sigmund Freud's quote "Love and work are the cornerstones of our humanness" as a basis of his definition. "To love and be loved is the foundation of a happy and emotionally filled life. Productive and hopefully meaningful work adds purpose, a sense of accomplishment and self-worth, and income to our lives. These are the building blocks to happiness and success in life." It was not long after I received his email that Larry, loved by his family and friends and admired and respected by everyone who knew him, died much too young, at the age of sixty-seven, of cancer.

Gary Pinsly, age sixty-two and the managing director of a wealth management company, also sent me his definition by email. "To live a life in God's favor by using his many blessings to treat others fairly, raise a healthy, strong family, be respected in the community, and offer help to those less fortunate. My personal wealth is always measured by the ability to look in the mirror daily knowing I have done the best I can possibly do under any circumstance. I can't find success unless I thank God daily for giving me the ability to comfort people when they are hurting, make them laugh when they need a lift, and give them hope when hope is diminished."

Nelda Fulghum, a sixty-four-year-old executive director of the McNeilly Center for Children in Nashville, responded to my question with several questions of her own. "The older I get, the more I think about how successful I am. I am continually asking myself the following questions: Did I love others, and did they love me? Did I make the world a better place for all who knew me? Did I teach my children to love and respect themselves and others, and did I inspire them to be the best they can be? Will God be happy with what I've done with my life?" One day when she looks back at her life, I hope she will be able to answer these questions in the affirmative.

Kathy Owen, a sixty-five-year-old senior executive assistant in the Nashville Metropolitan Transit Authority, wrote, "To me, a successful life has nothing to do with career but everything to do with relations and includes: To live in peace with one's self and with others, to know the love of family and friends, to know the joy and satisfaction of achievements, to know the transcending power of nature and the transcending power of faith."

Mark Goldfarb is a recently retired cardiologist and sixty-six years old. He sent me his definition while he was preparing to move to Utah to begin the next chapter in his life. "As a father, I believe success means seeing your kids happy, content, thriving, and independent but with solid roots and yet still recognizing and perhaps expressing appreciation for all you did in contributing to their success. As a physician, it means seeing children of patients you helped medically thank you some day for being at the right place at the right time and doing the right thing, with the result of saving a life and subsequently seeing the downstream effects on so many others and thereby truly making a positive difference in life. It also means having a partner who loves and supports you and always has your back and, even if you are not perfect, loves you anyway."

Dr. Griff Haber, a sixty-nine-year-old retired veterinarian, said, "One has had a successful life if when you are no longer alive, your family and friends still love and miss you and can say that their life is better, and they are a better person, because of you."

Owen Joyner is seventy years old and lists his profession as salesman. "I have been in sales in one form or another for my entire adult life." I sat down with Owen and his lovely wife, Amy, my neighbors for over twenty years. Owen wanted to go first. "My definition of a successful life is having a loving family and many close friends. My biggest success is having met and married Amy and then having our only child, who has given us a loving grandchild. My family is what makes me feel successful." Not completely satisfied with his answer, Owen added, "I would also like for someone to come up to me from time to time and tell me that I had touched them emotionally and had made a difference in their life. For me, that would add in making me feel successful."

His wife, Amy, sixty-eight and a retired financial industry developer, told me that when she was young, she had goals of making good grades, doing well in school, and making her parents proud. "As I grew older, success was defined as doing well in my business. But then the definition of success changed once again, and that remains my definition to this very day. It is that in my interactions with my family, friends, coworkers, and others I meet on the path of life, I have helped make them feel valued. That feeling of being of value is what results in a life of peace and joy."

My sister-in-law Nancy Hoffman, seventy years old, a community volunteer married to a physician and mother to three children, was quite specific in her response when I questioned her on her definition of a successful life. Nancy told me that "doing things you love to do, being with people you enrich and who enrich you, and raising happy, well-adjusted children is my definition."

Dr. Carl Zimmerman, a seventy-year-old expert in gynecology whom I have known for many years as a student and then colleague at VUMC, sent me his top ten ways to maximize the chance of living a successful life. From number ten to one here is his list:

10) Find ways to overcome obstacles that life places in your path.

9) Be a better listener than speaker. Everyone has a story worth learning about.

8) Always be willing to learn. The best teacher seems to be the best pupil.

7) Travel to random places to see things that you never expected to view or understand.

6) Read and view works of value, writing, art, and film.

5) Share what you can that is positive and good: knowledge, skills, empathy, love, and time.

4) Have a bucket list that challenges and rewards in equal proportion.

3) Continuously reset your life goals to a higher level.

2) Love. Hate and prejudice are cancers on success and limit happiness.

1) Surround yourself with positive people.

Carl added a bonus observation: "Success is like art; it cannot be defined, but you will recognize it when you see it." Carl has had his share of ups and downs in life, and these ten axioms have helped him look back on his life and consider it a most successful one.

Irwin Venick, a seventy-year-old experienced and well-respected attorney in Nashville, also gave me a list to help define what a successful life means to him. According to Irwin: "1) Create and maintain a good name. 2) Develop and use your innate and learned abilities. 3) Appreciate the skills and abilities you have employed in the world. 4) Develop and nourish loving relationships. 5) Provide adequate financial support for your family and community."

I met Steven S. Ohlman on one of my Uber drives to the airport in Chicago one cold winter day in 2020 and found him to be charming, thoughtful, and intelligent. He told me he was seventy-two years old and basically retired. When I told him I was writing a book on the definition of a successful life, he agreed to give me his definition. A few days later I received his definition by email. "My understanding of what makes a successful life hinges entirely on how well I am able to express my understanding of God. Many times, over the years, I have taken a wide road in life, impelled by materialistic desires. There were periods where I felt that I could never escape the darkness that I found myself encompassed in. No matter how desperate the situation, there was always a sliver of light. The tighter I held on to that light, the brighter that light came through, until I was able to rise above that so-called difficulty. In terms of material success, I have never become wealthy or powerful; however, I have a wonderful family, I have always had everything I needed, and I have learned that each experience in my life, whether good or bad, has shown me that God is everything."

Barbara Speller, a seventy-three-year-old civic volunteer, wife, and mother, told me that her formula for a successful life was in having a family with loving, close, respectful, and non-judgmental characteristics. "A life where you have been a good listener with a healthy dose of understanding, acceptance, forgiveness, and compassion—that is what a successful life is for me."

I met with Lee Stewart, a seventy-year-old data analyst and contract administrator at the Metro Social Services in Nashville, for his thoughts on the subject of a successful life. Here is what he told me: "At seventy, I've finally learned that a successful life involves equanimity in trying to maintain mental calmness, composure, and evenness of temper, especially when I feel under pressure with a difficult situation or person or dealing with a deadline." Clearly, this is an individual with a very specific singular definition of success but one that he has identified as the most important.

Barbara Jones, age seventy-one, a retired social worker, responded, "A successful life is one in which there is inner happiness. Many individuals continue to look for that feeling of happiness by attempting to achieve more contentment and peace. I define happiness as the ability to be satisfied with what you have and that you have been able to avoid the feeling of envy in your heart."

Another one of my colleagues, my friend Dr. Richard Porreco, is seventy-one years old and lives and works in Denver. "A successful life is one that has been purpose driven. It is in fulfilling that purpose where one can find satisfaction and success. A purpose can be one of art, music, gardening, or any number of other endeavors that gets you up in the morning and drives you to do something you love to do. A purposeful life is a successful life."

Richard's wife, Terese Kaske, sixty-one, also a physician, listened to her husband's definition and wanted to add her comments. "A successful life is to make a difference in someone's life in a positive way. Being able to help and support my family and patients makes me feel successful. Being good at what I do also makes me feel successful, as does having a loving and supportive husband who has enriched my life in so many ways."

Gil Fox III is seventy-two years old, married, with three grown daughters and three grandchildren. He is a retired businessman, entrepreneur, and estate planner. We have known each other for a very long time, and so I reached out to him to ask what his definition of a successful life was. Gil is a graduate of Colgate College and Vanderbilt Business School and has been an avid community volunteer in the Nashville Jewish and non-Jewish communities. Gil started our conversation with the comment, "I enjoy solving problems." This fact led him to list four items that contained his definition of a successful life, which he also admitted was very similar to his late father's definition of a successful life. His father, Gilbert Fox Jr., died at age ninety-eight. First on Gil's list is his commitment to providing for his family and binding them together as a close and loving family. Second concerned his commitment to maintaining a healthy body by doing regular exercise and eating a healthy diet, and third revolved around his faith. He works toward the continuation of the Jewish faith within himself, his family, and his community by promoting the spiritual, ethical, and cultural principles of Judaism. Finally, a successful life "is one in which I have been able to help others achieve a financial goal for themselves and their family." Gil did not hesitate to tell me that he believes he has fulfilled these four axioms and therefore was able to say, "I have lived a successful life."

Seventy-four years old and an educator and entrepreneur, Alan Fierstein sat down with me one December day in Boca Raton and was eager to share his opinions on the definition of a successful life. "A successful life is defined by how many people you have helped along the way." Alan and his wife had a daughter who died at a young age, and this stimulated their desire to reach out and help others by establishing a foundation. "As a young man, I was insecure and not a good student, but with the help of a mentor I found a way to become secure, more confident, and positive." He found it important to be a good father and husband, and these became critical aspects of a successful life. However, the loss of his daughter, Rachael, led him to realize that helping others was also a critical definition of a successful life. Once again, we witness an example of life's experiences and events helping to create what we envision to be our definition of a successful life.

A real estate agent, divorced, with two children, Nan Speller, age seventy-two, defines a successful life as one in which "you are able to put others before yourself. Life does not merely revolve around you; it revolves around others as well. Being successful also means that you have set goals for yourself and always are able to have something to look forward to." Nan was not completely satisfied with her answer and wanted to say more about her criteria for a successful life. "Money has had nothing to do with a successful life for me, because I have always had enough to take care of myself; however, success for me includes my community volunteer work that helps others. All in all, I believe I have lived a successful life based on this definition and that I did not let life's difficult downs drag me down with them. I am very proud that I was able to overcome the obstacles that life has thrown me."

Divorced, with two grown daughters, Dr. Steve Entman, a seventy-year-old retired OB/GYN with whom I worked with for over thirty years at VUMC, was quite specific in his definition. "My definition is threefold. First, it includes that I have focused on the values of others, understanding that people can have conflicting views, and that I have been respectful of others' way of life and values. Secondly, that I have had the experience of being delighted by my adult children as I have learned so much from them. Life as a father is an ongoing process as well as a cycle. And finally, that I have been able to have had the opportunity to express and receive love."

Alan Mazer, seventy-one years old and a lawyer in Nashville, told me that his definition of a successful life is one in which the individual: 1) takes on jobs that no one else wants to do, 2) puts heart and soul into seemingly trivial tasks, and 3) as a result of the first two, enriches the lives of others.

Also emphasizing the importance of making a difference in life in the overall definition of a successful life, Lee Kraft, a seventy-two-year-old principal of the Nashville accounting firm Kraft CPA, said that he would consider himself successful if, at the end of the day, he can say that he made a difference in a positive way to those who were important to him. Lee went on to add, "Professionally, it would also include being a productive, contributing member of our management team at our firm and a mentor to our younger team members and receiving expressions of gratitude from clients and friends who feel that I have helped them through their own challenges."

Lisa Small is seventy-two years old and a civic volunteer in Nashville. She wanted me to know that her definition of a successful life is one that is meaningful and joyful. By meaningful, Lisa means that an individual has contributed something of value to others, and by joyful she means the joy one has knowing that they will live on past their life on earth in the hearts of family, friends, and acquaintances.

Bob Dellaposta, very upbeat and cheerful, emailed me one paragraph that certainly indicated that he had fulfilled his definition of a successful life. "I am seventy-three and a part-time actor, a part-time professional trumpet player, a full-time music publisher, an adjunct professor at Nashville State Community

College, an evaluator for the Nashville Songwriters Association, and on staff at Songu.com, where I conduct online feedback critiques as a publisher. My life is successful because I wake up every morning and can't wait to get started doing something positive with my day. I end my day as I start it, looking ahead. I work seven days a week pitching songs around the world to artists, movies, television, and commercials. Success to me is finding things you love to do so much that you'd do them for free, and then finding a way to get paid for doing them."

Doris Shacklett was seventy-three years of age when she responded by email. Doris works at The Temple in Nashville as an administrative assistant and has held numerous jobs over her long career in office management, construction, banking, and special events. Although she attempted retirement for three months, she missed interactions with people and decided to take a job at The Temple. She has been happily married for fifty-six years and has two children, five grandchildren, and one recent great-grandchild. Doris stated that her father died when she was very young; however, because of her mother and grandparents, she stated, "I had the best childhood possible, and as an only child, I felt my world was pretty perfect." Doris wrote that "the biggest blessing in our lives has been our children and grandchildren." She was proud of the fact that all her children and all but the youngest grandchild have graduated from college, something she never accomplished. Having said all this, Doris wrote, "I do consider my life a success! I have discovered along the way that success can come in ways you never expected and that to me lifelong learning and being open to change were the keys to my success."

James Fishel, a seventy-five-year-old retired businessman and a lifelong friend of mine, brought up the subject of money and its relationship to success. "Achieving one's goals and aspirations contributes to living a successful life; however, acquiring money and possessions does not equate to being successful." He went on to add that "few people view their lives as successful unless their goals and aspirations are very simple ones." James, a very thoughtful man, had more to say about this subject. "A truly successful life lies in making a positive difference in your life as it affects your family, friends, and community and, in rare cases, the world."

Edna Jones, also seventy-five years old, is a Nashville Metro Government social worker and single mother. She was brief in her definition. "A successful life is one lived without too many regrets. You may, in hindsight, think you would have changed a few decisions; however, you would regardless have become the same person that you are now."

One very thoughtful response I received was sent to me by Rise L. Tucker, seventy years old and a retired teacher. She currently leads a rhythm band workshop for seniors in assisted living homes and memory care communities. "I believe all humans are destined for success since they are the product of the ultimate example of success, the moment of conception. When a sperm and ovum, quite by chance, unite to create a new life, what could be a more perfect example of success? From that moment on, every human being fights the odds of a continuous quest for success, nine months of fetal development, the harrowing trip down the birth canal, and that first breath outside the womb. Having accomplished all this, the infant lets out an urgent cry, announcing, 'I am here!' This cry is its first connection to the world, an innate form of communication that is perhaps the most important gift to his/her future success as a human being.

"The ability to connect with one's fellow man, and to turn that connection into acts and deeds that benefit not just oneself but others as well, also makes what I call a successful life. 'No man is an island.' 'Nothing exists in a vacuum.' 'If a tree falls in the forest and no one is there to hear it, does it make a sound?' These familiar quotes capture the essence of success-connection. The successful person must see him/herself in relation to others and as part of society. That society may be as small as family or as large as the world stage.

"The concept of success is a subjective matter, largely based on perspective. For better or for worse, society has established some common criteria for gauging success: amount of wealth, fame, celebrity, educational and professional degrees, and positions of authority, to name a few. By that criteria, one might conclude that a child born into poverty, who manages to finish high school, gets a minimum-wage job, and works his way through community college and gets a better job, then marries and has a family and supports that family is less a success than the Fortune 500 CEO who was born to millionaire parents. But I would suggest that their connection to society is different, but their success is equal. We can't always control the tools at our disposal in the quest for success. Sometimes there is access to money, higher education, an inborn talent, corporate support; the list of advantages is great. But the person who focuses on using the tools at hand and makes the most of these tools and then connects with others to the benefit of society is a successful person."

This group of individuals fifty to seventy-five years old has reached a stage in life where they have learned much from their earlier years as far as finding out what they love to do as a career or a vocation. They have been able to look backward in a retrospective manner and evaluate their lives, in a way that younger individuals are not as able to do. They can evaluate the important relationships in their lives such as the ones with their spouse, children, and family, as well as the close and nurturing friendships they have made along life's path. They can also evaluate whether their lives have made a positive difference in the lives of others. And with life expectancy now being in the late seventies for men and early eighties for women, it is also a time for critical reflections of what life has meant to them and if they had, by their definition, led a successful life.

The most frequently mentioned definition among this mature group of individuals was making the world a better place and making a positive impact on the lives of others. This definition was very closely followed by having a loving family and good friends. These definitions were then followed in decreasing frequency by having a strong religious faith, finding enjoyable work and career, accepting yourself for who you are, success by proxy, being grateful, having few regrets, being kind and respectful to others, having enough money to not have to struggle, living a purposeful life, educating yourself, and having a good reputation. Other definitions mentioned either once or twice by this group included having a calm and right mind, loving life, living a moral and ethical life, having wonderful memories, having a good sense of humor, being creative and tasting adventure, being a caring and forgiving person, having peace, having reasonable expectations, being able to take care of oneself, being in the moment, doing it "my way," taking care of one's body and mind, overcoming obstacles in life, beating back the demons of childhood, overcoming fear, and being happy.

CHAPTER 5

THE OLDER

"Always get a second opinion and make sure one of them is yours." Richard Feldman, friend

"A successful life is one when you have all you want." Steve Dansky, friend

"If you want to go fast, go alone. If you want to go far, go together." African Proverb

"The days are long, but the years are short." Gretchen Rubin

"Basically, when you get to my age, you will really measure your success in life by how many of the people you want to have love you actually do love you." Warren Buffett

THERE IS LITTLE AGREEMENT ON WHAT DEFINES AN older individual. When I was a young boy in the 1950s, my grandfather reached seventy years of age and was considered by all his family as quite old. Over the years, however, the older became those who had reached their eighties and certainly their nineties. There are currently approximately 1.9 million Americans who are in their nineties with an expectation that this figure will quadruple in the next ten years. For this category I have chosen individuals who are older than seventy-five years of age. These individuals have been able to experience life over a longer span of time than others much younger and are more able to look back at their lives and articulate their definitions of a successful life, and they're closer to being able to ascertain if they have indeed met their criteria and been successful.

One such individual was Sy Trachtman, age eighty-two, an unassuming, kind, soft-spoken, humble, and somewhat shy individual. Sy is a widower with two grown daughters and is a retired salesman of electronic equipment. After I asked him what he believed to be his criteria of a successful life, he began his response with the comment, "I don't believe I have achieved success yet." He then added that a successful life did not depend on money earned or accumulated, although he admitted that a certain level of money was necessary to survive and care for oneself and one's family. He stated after that, however, money did not define a successful life.

Even though he was hesitant to state that his life was successful, he told me that his definition centered around making a positive difference for others, including his family and community. He told me that he had worked for many years on social action committees and projects, visiting the elderly in nursing homes and contributing what little resources he could to worthwhile charities. He had done all this for most of his adult life and felt a sense of accomplishment and pride in these activities. Yet he still did not feel that he had led a successful life.

After listening to Sy's explanation of what he considered to be a successful life, I told him that I thought he had in fact met his criteria. He had made a difference in this world and the community by providing for his family and raising his daughters, who were productive young women in the community and who shared many of his moral and ethical values. In addition, he had spent countless hours to bring aid and comfort to those in need. Sy thought about this for a reflective moment and finally admitted that he had indeed met his criteria for a successful life by making a positive difference during his time on earth and thanked me for helping him understand that. I was touched by Sy's admission and realized that there are many of us who never define what we consider to be the elements of a successful life or properly ascertain if we have met our definition.

Some of what Sy told me was also expressed in my interview with a very close friend and successful businesswoman, Shirley Zeitlin, who was head of a large and prestigious real estate agency in Nashville. Shirley was eighty-four years old at the time of our interview, and I found her to be open and transparent in her remarks. Shirley has a beautiful smile and attitude toward life. She raised three boys, all of whom are good citizens of the Nashville community and who have given Shirley many wonderful grandchildren. In addition, Shirley is an active member of her Jewish community and a leader of many of its activities. She began our time together at her home stating that "a successful life is one in which you feel as if you have made a positive impact in people's lives and in particular with family and friends."

She went on to say that she had mentored many individuals in her business and felt that her advice had helped many of those she worked with. All this, she believed, contributed to her feeling of having had a positive impact on people's lives. Shirley added that this makes her feel as if she has led a successful life. She admitted that she'd had many challenges over her lifetime, but these strengthened her and opened the door to many opportunities that have enriched her life. Finally, she added, "My life has been a successful one mainly due to raising my children, having dear and loving friends, and helping others in need along the way." When I asked her how money affected her definition of success, she remarked that "money frees you to not have the stress of the lack of it. It frees you up to do for others, but it does not make you a better person or more successful."

Arnold Shapiro, at seventy-seven years of age, is a retired television producer of such hits as *Rescue 911* and *Big Brother*, and he won an Academy Award for his documentary *Scared Straight*. He is also the recipient of sixteen Emmy Awards. Arnold has been a close friend for the past fifty years and someone I consider to have used his creativity to become a very successful TV producer. "A successful life is one in which you ethically fulfill your dreams, goals, and ambitions; and one in which you contribute to the welfare of others, including people, animals, and the environment; and a life in which you gain wisdom to benefit yourself and share with others. A successful life must include living by the golden rule, being kind and thoughtful to others, and having a great deal of empathy and compassion; and that you are able to experience genuine happiness and give and receive love and not intentionally inflict physical or emotional pain on any person or living creature. And a successful life is one where you can experience, if not maximize, whatever talents, abilities, or gifts you possess, and that you are able to minimize the negative influences of guilt, disappointments, and mistakes so that negativity does not derail or depress you and that you can die without regrets."

I found Professor John Lachs, who was in his eighties when he agreed to an interview, most interesting. Dr. Lachs is a professor of philosophy at Vanderbilt University in Nashville, a position he has held for fifty-one years. John is a respected teacher and has had a very distinguished career. When I asked for his definition of a successful life, he immediately stated that success suggests having plans in life and that success is an achievement. He added that happiness is not an achievement but rather a result. He continued with an example. "Willy is a plumber and truly one of the happiest people I know. He is only interested in pipes, plumbing, and drinking beer. He has enough money to drink beer and live. His business success had afforded him to be able to be happy." Professor Lachs continued. "Success must be put into a time span. You need a past that allows for enough experiences to understand what true success is. It cannot be a single event like climbing Mount Everest. I think we overstate the notion of human nature. People are so different from each other, and because of this, we have so many different values. So, there will be many different definitions of what a successful life truly is."

Dr. Lachs then spoke to me about desire and how it is desire that leads to action and satisfaction. "You do the best you can to achieve something, but it does not necessarily bring satisfaction." He cited examples such as choosing the wrong profession, the wrong vacation, the wrong companion or partner, or the wrong house in which to live. Finally, he began to answer the initial question. "My definition is based on the notion that a successful life means many different things to many different people, often based on their age and life experiences. My ultimate definition is to have been able to achieve what I wanted and that there were enough challenges left in my life to have something to which I could look forward." I felt as if he had more to say about this, and so I asked him about the role luck had in being able to live a successful life. He clearly felt that luck played a very important role in his life and stated, "I have lived eighty-four years, and that is proof alone of my luck."

He gave another example as to how luck played a role in his life when he met his wife by chance at a theater in Vienna that he had not wanted to attend but was urged to go to by his mother. That encounter led to a long and loving marriage that only ended recently with his wife's death. "Luck presents the opportunity, but you have to seize that opportunity. One of people's biggest mistakes is not being able to distinguish between short- and long-term consequences, due to the pleasure that comes in the short run but is disastrous in the long run." He added, "If only we could readily do the right thing and understand the long-term consequences. We want the short-term pleasure, such as smoking, but ignore the long-term effects." Interestingly, as we concluded our time together, Dr. Lachs had one more thing to add. "If you do not believe you had a successful life, but your children have, you could believe that you have had a successful life by proxy."

Billy Hudson is seventy-eight years old and has been a professor of medicine and biochemistry at Vanderbilt University Medical Center for the past eighteen years. I met Billy at a dinner party in 2019 and told him about the book I was putting together, at which time he made a few interesting comments that made me believe he would be quite interesting to interview. I was right. Billy has a story about his life that needs to be told. As a young child, Billy was emotionally, physically, and sexually abused and tortured, and yet he emerged from these adverse experiences with a desire to help others who'd had similar situations, as well as a strong desire to use his professional role in the advancement of science. "I am a survivor of child abuse from both parents and am fortunate to be here." Billy was born in Pine Bluff, Arkansas, and reared in the tiny rural community of Grapevine, Arkansas. At age sixteen and as a high-school dropout, he was rescued from his abusive family situation by a teacher who helped him enter college and remove himself from a life of agony. He was a motivated student, and after graduating from Henderson State Teachers College, a place he calls his foster home, he obtained a master's degree in biochemistry at the University of Tennessee and then a PhD at the University of Iowa. After a stint in the army and postdoctoral studies at Harvard Medical School, Billy settled down to a life of rigorous scientific research, which he continues to this very day.

Billy told me that the loving atmosphere of the world of education and university life has given him the strength to go on with life and a reason to live. "My success comes from two things. First, I was good at science, which was and still is my anchor in life, and helps explain why, even at the age of seventy-eight, I continue to do medical research. It brings purpose to my life. Since I was nine years old, I knew that I had to rescue my brother and sister, and it was later I would learn that I have a strong drive to help others as well. My purpose is to help those who are suffering from the aftermath of adverse childhood experiences and those who are less fortunate than I am. I have applied my love of science to help others. The drive that gives me that purpose to help others is the second definition of what makes my life feel successful."

Billy is married to Julie, a pediatric anesthesiologist, and together they have three productive children, all of whom work in the field of science. For the past ten years, Billy and Julie have run the Aspirnaut™ Summer Research Internship, a program for aspiring voyagers, which they founded. The program brings high-school students from around rural America to Vanderbilt for six weeks to experience science research and to receive professional guidance and mentorship for self-discovery, wellness, and career planning, a road that Billy traveled from early life.

Billy is so very proud of this program, which allows him to feel successful in his lifelong quest to help others. Billy is emblematic of the objective definition of a successful life. He was able to minimize his extremely negative genetic and environmental influences to create a life of success.

I'd wanted to interview Dr. David Barton ever since I began writing this book. I have known David since the early 1970s when both of us were Vanderbilt University Medical Center faculty members, and I noticed then that he was a gifted and highly intellectual psychiatrist, frequently expressing cutting-edge views. He was passionate about educating students of medicine about death and dying, a subject that was in its infancy in medicine at that time. David is married to Lynn, also a therapist, and together they have three children, two of whom are also psychiatrists and one who is an attorney.

David was eighty-three years old at the time we spoke by phone, rather than in person, because we were both in precautionary isolation due to the coronavirus pandemic. David was born in Selma, Alabama, attended the University of Alabama, and received his MD degree at Tulane University, following which he completed a residency in psychiatry at Charity Hospital in New Orleans, Louisiana. After serving in the army at Fort Hood, Texas, David joined the University of Virginia Medical Center for two years then came to Nashville to join the faculty at Vanderbilt University Medical Center, where he reorganized the student teaching program in psychiatry and was able to focus his attention on issues surrounding death and dying. In 1974, David and a Vanderbilt colleague helped found Alive Hospice, which was then the first hospice in the southeast and third in the country. This community-supported, not-for-profit hospice continues to this day to be an important facility for end-of-life patients.

"I have always felt a desire to help medical students' and practitioners' ability to better understand and approach the issues of loss, grief, and the process of dying and death in caring for their patients." With his teaching and writings, David became a pioneer and expert on how the medical profession dealt with the subject of death and dying. "A successful life to me is incorporated into our identity and strivings as we develop, and which has an internal as well as an external component. The internal component is how we define ourself in terms of success, and the external comes from how we see others as viewing the nuances of our success. I believe success is found in the realization of meaning in our lives, and meaning, to me, is the very structure of our sense of aliveness. My meaning and my sense of aliveness is derived from several of my life's components or activities, as I like to call them.

"The first component is my biological self, the activity of my maintaining a healthy physical self to be able to participate in the activities of my life. Second is experiencing authentic aliveness in the interpersonal activity with everyone I encounter, for having good relationships is critical to a meaningful and successful life. The third dimension is found in developing a healthy psychological being, with that activity being manifested in the ability to deal positively and adapt to the frustrations and obstacles that we all encounter in life. Fourth, meaning comes from my activity in the sociocultural context: the activity within my marriage, having children, living in Nashville, being a physician, being Jewish, and that which comes from a host of other factors that make up my day-to-day existence. Finally, my meaning comes from my philosophical views and my having embraced significant spiritual activity in my life, my relationship with God, and my religion. All five areas are intertwined and come together to create a sense of wholeness and meaning."

Not quite finished, David added, "Maintaining authenticity, which means being true to how I represent myself, staying connected to the now and thereby relevant, being creative, and continually learning. These are all activities of my being which are critical for me to view my life as meaningful and successful. To me being successful means that I am a work in progress. I still have many choices to make; therefore, I truly do not know if I can say I am successful yet, because I have not yet lived my entire life."

I reached out to my teacher and mentor during my training in obstetrics and gynecology at Yale New Haven Hospital for his definition of a successful life. Dr. Edward J. Quilligan is one of this country's most well-known and respected teachers and scientists in the field of high risk pregnancies. At age ninety-four, although now retired, he is still active and leading a relatively full life. "The definition of success that makes the most sense to me was having goals and achieving them. I had a family and a professional goal. The goal for the family was to be a good father, and I think with lots of help from my wife, Betty, I have achieved that goal. We have six children who are not only successful but good people. My professional goal was to be a good physician and teacher, and with the help of many students and residents, I think I have achieved success in my professional goal. That success is measured by the wonderful achievement of the young people of whose education I have had the privilege to be some small part of." These comments are indicative of a truly great and humble man.

Father Joseph Breen, a retired priest in Nashville and a well-known and respected man of God, was kind enough to respond to my question. Here is his response: "I am now eighty-three years old and perhaps wiser than before on what constitutes a successful life. 'What can I do for you' is part of an attitude that makes good friends and gives one much joy and satisfaction. Another thing that is part of a successful life is to pray that you will always do your best and do what is right. Another important ingredient is to take time to reflect on this wonderful world God has created for us: the magnificent stars at night, the many planets, and the great order of our universe; to appreciate the diversity in our world, the beautiful colors and varieties of flowers in the field and fish in the ocean, the great number of birds in our skies, and all the animals that dwell on our lands; to have the great joy of knowing people of foreign lands and different religious beliefs; to reflect and be grateful for the birth of a baby, truly one of God's great miracles; to believe in God who made us in His image and likeness; finally, to worship Him with a loving community. These are the things and ways that make a successful life, one filled with blessed memories, much happiness, and love."

Alan Rose is a seventy-six-year-old former hotel executive,

married with two grown boys and now retired in Jacksonville, Florida. He has been a friend of mine for over sixty years, and so I wanted to hear his definition of a successful life. "A successful life is to leave the world a little better than when I entered it and to have lived by the Boy Scouts' laws." I asked him what those laws were and without hesitation, having been a Boy Scout many years earlier, Alan listed them from memory. "They are being trustworthy, loyal, helpful, friendly, courteous, kind, obedient, cheerful, thrifty, brave, clean, and reverent."

I had looked forward to interviewing one of my dearest and oldest friends, seventy-nine-year-old retired dentist Larry Averbuch. We met in kindergarten. Larry had this to say. "A successful life to me is in the eye of the beholder. In other words, how you view yourself as a good and decent human, raising good children, being a good spouse, living an honest and ethical life, and giving back to the community in which you live. That is all there is to it. You do not need money or fame. You just need to be a good person."

Another seasoned and experienced individual, Dr. Louis Levy is a seventy-seven-year-old retired pediatrician whom I have known since we were teenagers, and who was my roommate while we attended Vanderbilt Medical School. Louis's definition, which he described as having multiple dimensions, included "fulfilling purpose for aspects of my life as a Jewish man, a father, a doctor, and a family man. For family, it means that I nurtured my children, gave and received love from them, and that they were happy. In terms of my religion, I found purpose by participating in Tikkun Olum"—which means in

Hebrew "to repair the world"—"and in terms of my community, it is to make a difference in people's lives, which I felt I did as a physician." He finally concluded with this: "My definition will probably change as I grow even older. I would like to add to my definition that it also means being able to die well."

Jeanne Youngkins is a retired Vanderbilt University Medical Center employee who is the only person I have ever met who shares my exact birthday. She was seventy-eight years old when I asked her to send me her definition of a successful life. "There are so many definitions of what it means to have lived a successful life. Few of us will be defined by historians as being successful, but perhaps it is in our daily interactions where true success lies. What makes each of us successful is how we interact with others. Often, I feel frustrated when there is suffering in the world that I am unable to alleviate. However, I can make a difference each day through my interactions with those around me. By listening to and caring for my family, truly listening to a friend, or simply smiling at another person in the grocery aisle, I am given the opportunity to be supportive and uplifting. I believe that it is in these exchanges that we are following the directive to love one another. If we do this, then no matter the pluses or minuses in our lives, we will be successful."

Annette Eskind is ninety-two years old and a long-retired social worker, wife of the late physician and humanitarian Dr. Irwin Eskind, and mother of two sons, both of who are prominent physicians in Nashville. She has also been a civic volunteer and has done much to improve the welfare of her community. Annette told me that when she was young, she dreamed of becoming a ballerina, which was something her parents wished for her as well. "To become a ballerina in those days would certainly have been my definition of success." However, as she grew older and realized that becoming a ballerina was not to be, she discovered her real passion was in social work and dedicated her life to the welfare of others through the profession of social work.

It was not difficult for Annette to define a successful life for herself nor difficult to admit that she had indeed been successful. "A successful life is one in which I have helped others in need as they struggled with life's difficult problems. My other goal in life was to be a loving wife to the man I loved dearly and to raise our sons to be good citizens. All that has happened, and I can honestly say that my life has been a successful one."

I spent a most interesting afternoon with Phyllis Alper, also ninety-two years old and in excellent health. Phyllis was married for fifty-eight years to a prominent physician in Nashville, and together they had two daughters. Phyllis also has four grandchildren and two great-grandchildren as well as a very large family that includes thirty-four first cousins. Phyllis is petite, amazingly frenetic, loquacious, and spry—and eager to let me know that her life has been very full and rewarding. She began dancing at age three and for many years taught all types of dancing, including ballet, tap, and ballroom. She worked in her father's store following college for approximately twenty years, when she turned her energies to her family and community service.

Phyllis exclaimed to me that she is so blessed to have a large, loving family and that nothing was more important to her than to maintain a close and nurturing relationship with all her large number of relatives. "I have truly been blessed to have the family I have, and I am grateful for my good health and the love I receive from family and friends." Phyllis is not content with a life of inactivity. At age eighty, Phyllis took up oil painting and now sells many of her paintings and hangs dozens of them throughout her beautiful home in Nashville. In addition, she told me that she does crossword puzzles each day and reads at least one book a week. Phyllis also told me that people need to appreciate what they have and not keep wanting more and that money and fame were not important to living a successful life. What was important to this most energetic lady was to do for others and leave something of value behind. "I thank God every night that I had the husband I had and lived the life I have lived. My definition of a successful life is one that embraces the love of my family and friends and a life of making a positive difference in the lives of others. In that regard, my life has been a successful one."

Bernie Strassner has lived across the hall from me and my wife in Boca Raton, Florida, for the past thirty years, so I wanted to reach out to him for his definition of a successful life, as he had certainly lived a long and productive one. At ninety-two, Bernie is a retired civil engineer who lives most of the year in New York City. He and his late wife, Bernice, raised two daughters and have three grandchildren. Several cardiovascular strokes in the last two years have left him unable to walk and take care of himself, so he has a home health aide who lives with him to allow for a winter in the warmth of South Florida.

"My definition of a successful life is best defined by one

word: persistence. You have to set a goal and then dedicate yourself to achieving that goal." I asked Bernie what his goal was. "My goal was to take care of my family. That was my primary goal and included my wife and children as well as my mother who was widowed at a young age. I had no choice but to be successful financially to be able to achieve that primary goal." The many pictures of his family scattered around Bernie's apartment offered ample evidence of the importance Bernie placed on his family as a marker of a successful life. I then asked Bernie if he had lived a successful life by his definition. His response was sobering. "I guess I can say that I have lived a successful life by that definition; however, now with Bernice gone as well as all my friends, it is difficult for me to view the life ahead of me as successful."

Lou Bass, at ninety-six, was equally focused on the fact that money did not equal success but that it freed you from the stress of survival and allowed you the opportunity to do for others. Lou was clearly an entrepreneur, having gone from working in his father's clothing store to becoming a founder of Humana Health. Lou said that when he grew up, his family was not rich, but he never felt poor. He learned from his father that to help others in need was an important part of a life well spent, so it was no surprise to him that he became philanthropic as he acquired wealth, giving millions of dollars to a variety of worthwhile institutions and causes. Lou's definition of a successful life rested on the foundation of being content with oneself, having and reaching a goal in life, and pleasing others along the way, which to him meant being empathetic toward family, friends, and employees.

"Life is a journey, one that we are not sure how it is going to turn out. But overall, based on that definition, I believe I have lived a successful life."

Waldi Mizell is eighty-nine years old and someone I have known for a very long time, as she lives both in Nashville and Boca Raton, Florida. I sat down with her one January afternoon in 2020 to find out what she thought was the definition of a successful life. Waldi was born in Germany in 1930 and lived through the tumultuous and tragic times of World War II as a young child and teenager. She told me that she was very lucky to have had affluent, loving, and wonderful parents who watched over her and had her live with them until she was thirty-two. During that time, she obtained a college degree in language and gained employment at NATO, a job she truly loved. She met her first husband, Frank, on the *Queen Elizabeth* cruise ship. He was from Canada, and so she moved to his country after they got married. After Frank died, Waldi took over his three companies, eventually selling all three. She became an American citizen in 1986 when she met her second husband, Rudy, in Florida, who died some thirteen years later. Finally, Waldi met Andy, her third and last husband. They had a wonderful marriage; however, once again tragedy struck when he died of a sudden heart attack.

While Waldi has no children of her own, she told me that she had many stepchildren and a huge family in Germany. "A successful life to me first and foremost is one in which I have a large number of friends and family whom I love and who also love me." But there was more that Waldi wanted to say about her definition. "I try to always do the right thing in life, and one of those things is to help others in need. I have given of my resources to a large variety of individuals and causes, such as the YMCA, that were helpful in one way or another. When I die, I want to feel that I have helped others who needed aid and encouragement. I am lucky to be able to have helped others." Waldi ended our interview by saying, "Because I have a large number of friends and family and because I have been lucky enough to be able to help others in need, I believe my life has been a successful one."

Rusty Groffman is seventy-six years old and confined to a wheelchair due to severe neuropathies and severe arthritis. Her companion is her dog, Kelev, who picks up items she drops to the floor. She has had her share of problems in life. Divorced when she was eight months pregnant with twins, Rusty struggled to deal with the death of one of her twin girls after birth and the challenges of raising a child who was visually impaired. At age forty-five, she was diagnosed with advanced breast cancer and underwent a difficult time with treatment and its many serious side effects; however, somehow, she survived these particular challenges. Her daughter eventually married and gave Rusty two "beautiful granddaughters." Rusty told me that "in spite of the challenges on this rocky road called life, I managed to help nurture three drop-dead beautiful girls who have grown up to be good, smart, honest, and productive citizens. I am a survivor and am grateful to be here to talk about it. Because of this, I believe my life is a successful one despite all its problems." Rusty's definition of a successful life, therefore, includes success by proxy, being grateful, and being able to deal with adversity.

Betty Lee Rosen, age seventy-seven, boiled it down to a very simplistic and different definition than I had heard from others. "The key to a successful life is a long and happy marriage." Not a definition for all, but certainly for her it was a definitive definition. She and her husband, Howard, have been married for over fifty years.

Her husband, Howard Rosen, an eighty-year-old retired physician in good health and active in his community, also viewed a successful life in terms of his family. "A successful life is about marrying the right partner: one who has a good sense of humor and self-esteem, is thoughtful, kind, fair, and wise; one who believes in you, represents and advises you well, and is a model for your children; and one who is able to help solve the challenges that are inevitable in a lifetime." In that sense, he exclaimed, "I have had a successful life."

Jim Harris, seventy-seven years old and a retired lawyer as well as my friend for the past forty-seven years and a neighbor who often joins me for evening cocktails, told me that his definition of a successful life was quite simple. "My definition is best demonstrated by an inverted pyramid, with the base representing birth and my youth years. As I traveled through life, the sides of the pyramid expand and represent family, profession, personal growth, and many other aspects of my life. Finally, at the top of this inverted pyramid, the mountaintop is the place I stand and look downward with pride and a feeling of a job well done. Most of all, however, this mountaintop view allows me to understand that my life has been a successful one because of being able to love others and being loved. That is my overarching definition of a successful life."

Sylvia Shepard, our family matriarch at age eighty-five, also focused on her family to define a successful life. "If you are happy, your family is happy, and if you are all connected as a family, then your life has been a successful one."

Jerry Kline, a retired eighty-six-year-old dentist, mirrored some of these values regarding family and a successful life. "A successful life for me is having three children who have all grown up to be successful." He added, "Having a joyful, loving wife for fifty-seven years, who has been a role model for our children, is also part of my definition of a successful life." Jerry, however, did not stop there. "Having good friends and being able to maintain a positive attitude are also critical factors in living a successful life."

Mickey Westman, age eighty, had this to say: "To live a successful life is to be able to deal with the ups and downs of life, to be a good person who is kind, considerate, and respectful of others, and then to pass these values on to others, especially your children."

A successful music producer of such groups as Doctor Hook, Ron Haffkine, eighty, told me that "the best thing that happened to me on my path to living a successful life was when I became infected with the polio virus as a teenager." Polio resulted in Ron being paralyzed and requiring years of therapy—some of it in Warm Springs, Georgia. "Polio actually strengthened my resolve to do something productive with my life and helped me to realize that I can overcome adversity," which Ron did. He went on to also spend much of his time and resources to help others. Ron told me that "a successful life is one in which you have a job or career you enjoy, have good friends that you trust and care deeply about, and have someone you love and who also loves you." He added that "money is not important after you have enough to pay for the necessities of life."

Jimmy Small is eighty-eight years old and a successful businessman. He has a wonderful wife of over fifty years, four successful children, and many grandchildren and great-grand-children. In good health, Jimmy loves to fish and spend time with his family. He has also been a significant contributor to the social welfare of his community. His response on what constitutes a successful life was emblematic of individuals in their eighties. "A successful life is one in which you take care of the responsibilities that you incur as well as being able to give back to your community by giving as much of your time and resources possible to help others in need."

Betsy Chernau is eighty-two years old and one of the most energetic and vivacious persons I have known since high school days. She has an infectious personality and knows no strangers. I was, therefore, grateful when she sent me her definition of a successful life. "Success can be quite personal and many different things to many people. For me, attitude and thinking of others has so much to do with having success. I have told my grandkids that to talk less and listen more, to give of themselves without thinking, 'What is in it for me?' *that* is true success. I was told in my high-school yearbook that my ambition in life was to lead a contented and successful life by making others happy. To this day, if I can put a smile on someone's face, I am successful. If I can say one small thing to help someone feel better, I am successful. If I can donate my time to help my family, friends, and community, even in a small way, I am successful. I am still trying to make my life have purpose and meaning and to make a positive imprint one day at a time and one person at a time. This place we call community is a metaphor for a campsite. We are only here for a short time. While we are here, we take advantage of it, use it, enjoy it, and benefit from it. Therefore, we are obligated to take good care of it, and as with a campsite, we must make certain that when we leave, we leave it not just as we found it but better off than when we arrived. That is my definition of a successful life."

A retired and successful lawyer, Ted Pailet, eighty-two years of age, told me that the first thing that came to his mind regarding my question was being content with one's lot in life. But then he had second thoughts. "Having at least one close and good friend to whom one can bare one's soul, having unconditional love of family, being bereft of grudges and jealousy, that is my definition."

Sally Levine was ninety-one years old when I spent an hour at her independent living apartment on a very hot September day in Nashville. Sally has been a widow for thirty-eight years, has two sons and two grandchildren, and has spent most of her adult life as a civic volunteer. She is a graduate of Northwestern University majoring in journalism and a past employee in her husband's factory many years ago. Sally told me that a successful life is totally defined by the individual and then stated that when she sees a wrong, she then sees what can be done about it. She added that nothing is ever finished, that no matter what you do, there are a million other things to do and to take care of. She was an active and longtime member of the League of Women Voters and told me that she had played a small role in some endeavors but not all. She had also been quite active in supporting the Nashville Symphony and the arts community of Middle Tennessee. Her definition of a successful life is knowing that when she saw something was wrong, she began working to correct it; however, she was reluctant to say that her life has been a complete success. Rather, she told me that her achievements have been episodic, and on some occasions, she had been successful, but not always.

"My success has been spotty, but that is my personality to not speak of my successes in life." It was interesting to me that such an accomplished woman who had done so much over many years to make this world a better place and whose definition of a successful life was the knowledge that when she saw a problem in life, she would attempt to fix it, still could not bring herself to admit that she had led what she would call a completely successful life. Sally is certainly a humble woman.

Howard Levy, eighty years old, has been a close friend since I was twenty-one. He was beginning law school as I was starting medical school. Divorced and the father of three daughters, one of whom died many years ago, Howard is a retired businessman and spends his time traveling between homes in Palm Beach, Florida, the Hamptons, New York, and Nashville. Howard told me that his definition of a successful life was threefold. First is being a good father, which he feels he has been, and second is living as stress-free a life as possible. "Stress kills, and I avoid it as much as I can by staying away from controversial issues.

Having a stress-free life is critical to a successful life." The third definition of a successful life is having a few truly close friends. "Close, loving friends are the foundation of a successful life, and I have those in my life, and so after all I have been through in my life, I feel successful."

In reviewing what this group of people over seventy-five years of age had to say about a successful life, I find it interesting that making a positive impact on other lives and in the community once again led the list of definitions, followed by finding love, having a loving family and friends, and fulfilling dreams and goals. Other comments this older group mentioned in decreasing frequency include being grateful, being a good person, living by the Golden Rule, success by proxy, being able to deal with adversity, appropriately using gifts of talent and abilities, being happy, having blessed memories, living by the Boy Scout creed, having a job you enjoy, putting a smile on someone's face, being content with what you have, and avoiding stress. As one reaches this later milestone of life, people are reflective and able to look back to determine whether they feel their lives have been successful.

We evaluate and measure so many things in our lives that I was somewhat surprised to discover just how few people stop to consider whether they have led a successful life. Most of the individuals in this book admitted they hadn't given it much thought. However, once they were asked the question, they were all quite interested in sharing with me both their definitions as well as whether they felt they had achieved their personal definition. One individual told me that she began asking her friends and

family about this subject, and it engendered a healthy and vig-
orous discussion each time. Peter Eagle Sims, editor of *Silicon
Guild* and the author of *What is Success* on the internet, wrote,
"After studying leadership and ethics at Stanford, I became con-
vinced that the question 'What is Success?' is the best question
anyone can ask themselves, young or old, over and over and over
again."

All this led me to believe that all of us should, from time
to time, as we age, evaluate what it is that we believe are the
components of a successful life and whether we are on the right
path to fulfill that definition. Hopefully, by age seventy-five, an
individual has thought about this and attempted to measure his
or her life in terms of success.

CHAPTER 6

A PERSONAL
POINT OF VIEW

*"All those days that came and went, little did I
know that they were life."* Stig Johansson

*"There is said to be three great spiritual questions:
Who am I? Why am I here?
How am I to live my life?"* Frank Powell

"Humility is our greatest virtue." David Brooks

*"Without pain there is no growth. Without growth there is
no pain. Without either there is no life."* Frank H. Boehm

AFTER READING AND LISTENING TO MORE THAN
two hundred definitions of what constitutes a successful life, I
was ready to consider my own definition. Initially, I began by
using the generic and more objective definition of being able to
maximize my genetic potential and environmental influences. I
was fortunate to have been raised by loving and caring parents.
As an only child, I received a great deal of attention as well as
accolades from the two most important and influential people
in my young life, so I believe that the nurturing environment in
which I was raised was clearly maximized due to these circumstances. Being told that I was wonderful and special throughout
my childhood contributed to my becoming a secure adult with
few anxieties.

When you are unconditionally loved and supported in a nurturing way, it is not surprising that you are more likely to reach
for goals that otherwise might seem unattainable. My parents
were middle class, my mother a housewife and my father a clothing salesman. I went to public schools, took a yearly two-week
family vacation each summer to Miami Beach, Florida, rode my
bike with neighborhood friends, and participated in sports. I was
far from wealthy, but I never felt poor.

The confidence I gained as a child and young man enabled
me to do so many of the things I eventually did in life. No one
in my family had attained an education beyond college, yet even

though I was not the smartest student, I reached beyond that by deciding to go to medical school. That confidence was the tool that led to my becoming a physician, which was one of the most important decisions I made in life.

I also believe that I was able to maximize the genetic potential given to me by my parents. Their story is an important one to tell, as it helps explain my belief that I was able to maximize my genetic potential. My parents were educated in Germany and did not attain the equivalent of an American college degree. However, both had wonderful common sense and understood what was important in life. I believe the main gift I received from my parents, and in particular my father, was the gift of vision. It was my father's vision that led him to understand that he and my mother had to leave Germany in 1938 to escape Nazi Germany. This took incredible courage and vision, which I believe my father passed on to me and became embedded in my DNA.

On January 30, 1933, Adolf Hitler became chancellor of Germany, and for the next twelve years, his reign would cause unimaginable crimes against humanity. My parents, Ludwig and Ilse Boehm, were born and raised in Germany and were witness to the rise of Nazi Germany and the evil that resulted. They were among a group of German Jews who survived these crimes, and as a young man, I often wondered how they knew they needed to leave their home, family, and friends as well as their business and immigrate to America.

How was it that my father, only thirty years old when Hitler took over the government in Germany, understood that he could no longer live in the land of his ancestors and needed to move to a strange country? Over the years, my father and I had many conversations about his decision to leave Germany. It was his faith, vision, and courage that not only changed his and my mother's lives but also resulted in monumental life-altering events for the Boehm family.

In 1935, Germany passed the Nuremberg laws, which all but denied any element of citizenship to the Jewish population. The laws prohibited Jews from marrying or having sexual relations with persons of German non-Jewish blood, and most political and citizen rights were abolished. Jews now needed to carry identity cards stamped with a red *J* along with new middle names for all Jews who did not have clearly identifiable Jewish names. Males had the name "Israel" stamped on their cards, and "Sara" was stamped on female cards, making it quite easy for police to know who was Jewish and who was not. The Nuremberg laws created a real problem for my father.

At that time, my father was in a relationship with a non-Jewish woman, but should his relationship be discovered by the authorities, he would be arrested and imprisoned. It was late one evening in 1935 when my father and his lover, asleep in her apartment, were awakened by the siren of a Gestapo wagon. My father looked down on the street and saw several Gestapo (German State Police) officers running into their building and racing up the stairs. As he quickly dressed, feeling the pounding of his heart, he heard the policemen run past his girlfriend's door, arresting another Jewish male down the hall who was also involved with a non-Jewish German woman.

As Ludwig watched them take the man away in handcuffs,

he knew he had dodged a dangerous bullet. He quickly finished dressing, tenderly held and kissed his lover goodbye, and ended their relationship. It was just too dangerous. Sadness filled his heart and tears began to appear on his cheeks. What was going to happen to him and his family? What was going to happen to the Jews of his beloved country?

My father told me that his father, Heinrich, was a strict disciplinarian who demanded obedience and a dedication to study and hard work. Heinrich was a typical German of his time, and while he was not one to dwell on the emotional side of life, he was careful to stress a need for his three sons to live an honorable and ethical life as well as one that carefully viewed the world with discerning eyes. He told his son after his twelfth birthday that one of the most important things he could do in life was to not follow others blindly but rather to carefully evaluate what would be right for him. Heinrich stressed that following the herd mentality could have serious negative effects. He wanted Ludwig to think for himself.

This was a vital lesson and legacy Heinrich would leave for his son Ludwig. Heinrich Boehm would die prior to his youngest son becoming a Bar Mitzvah the following year, but Ludwig would never forget the advice his father had given him. It was advice my father would give to me many years later.

My father loved his Judaism. He enjoyed the teachings and the culture of this most ancient of religions. As he aged, he would attend many Friday night services at his synagogue and celebrate all the major Jewish holidays, something he continued to do until the day he died at age eighty-five. My father told me that being

Jewish and living a life filled with Jewish culture and tradition made him feel peaceful. Living a life without the ability to practice and celebrate Judaism was not an option for Ludwig, and this helped my father make one of the most important decisions of his life, a decision that demanded vision.

After Ludwig and his lover broke off their relationship, he began to make frequent short trips to Nuremberg to meet young, single Jewish women at weekend garden parties held for the purpose of meeting suitable partners. It was at one of these parties that he met my mother, a young, beautiful Jewish woman. He was immediately attracted to her. She had a most wonderful, dimpled smile and a pleasing personality, and he was clearly smitten.

Although Ilse was not so sure at first, Ludwig knew he wanted to make her his wife. Eventually after several times together with friends and family, she too fell in love with this most charming and persistent man, and a wedding was planned. There was one thing, however, that Ludwig knew he had to tell Ilse as they made their plans to wed. He needed to let her know that he had already begun to make plans to leave Germany and move to America.

My parents were wed on December 25, 1935, in Nuremberg. This day was chosen as it was all but certain that the Nazis and Gestapo would be at home with their families celebrating Christmas and, therefore, would leave German Jews alone, even if for only a short twenty-four hours. My parents had an uneventful wedding that day and partied well into the night. It was the last time they would have such a luxury in Germany.

Anti-Semitism was not new to Germany, and my father had seen much of this coming. He had attended a Hitler speech given several years prior to 1933 in Bamberg and heard him speak of the evil Jew and how Jews were the root cause of Germany's crumbling economy. My father told me that he had read portions of Hitler's book *Mein Kampf* ("My Struggle"), and learned of his hatred for the Jewish people. He knew then that this was a man who would, if given power, use that power to inflict much pain and anguish upon Jews in Germany. With Hitler now in power, Ludwig understood that Germany could no longer be considered a place for Jews to live a spiritual, peaceful, or productive life.

Leaving Germany, however, was not an easy task for my parents. They had to leave their home in Bamberg without being compensated and could only arrange for a small amount of prefabricated furniture, which fit into a specific-sized wooden crate arranged much as a Rubik's Cube, to accompany them to America. As Jews leaving Germany could not take money or worthwhile possessions, my mother and father took what cash they had along with the jewelry they possessed, put it into a bag, attached a large stone to the bag, and in the still of night threw it into a river in Nuremberg rather than allow these valuables to wind up in the hands of Nazis.

Ludwig and Ilse left Germany by train to Holland. They boarded The T.S.S. *Statendam* in Amsterdam, settled in their second-class cabin, and began their long journey across the Atlantic Ocean, arriving in New York City Harbor on August 28, 1938. As they stood holding hands on the bow of the ship overlooking the harbor, tears filled their eyes as they passed the Statue of Liberty, a monument of freedom on which was inscribed the famous words by Emma Lazarus, a Jew: "Give me your tired, your poor, your huddled masses yearning to breathe free."

Jews who very early envisioned a Germany in which they were no longer welcomed belonged to a group of individuals who possessed a clear vision of what was happening to their country. Sadly, many German Jews did not have the resources, contacts, will, or vision to leave their native home. It was my father's vision and contacts in America that allowed for him and his wife to survive, which eventually led to my birth on April 11, 1940, in Nashville, Tennessee.

My birth led to the birth of my three children, Todd, Thomas, and Catherine, and their births were followed by children of their own: Riley, Adam, Marly, Seth, Max, Sam, Gabriel, Lucy, and Eden. The actions Ludwig Boehm took while still a young man allowed for the addition of thirteen Jews into a current world Jewish population of only sixteen million. There is a Jewish saying that he or she who saves one life has saved all humanity. Clearly, Ludwig Boehm had fulfilled that prophecy.

It is this vision that my parents possessed that helped me understand that my definition of a successful life rested, in part, on the fact that they had given me the genetic tools to display my own version of vision. That vision led me to choose the field of medicine as my profession. It led me to have the vision to understand the potential of a new and exciting sub-specialty in obstetrics and gynecology called maternal fetal medicine and to then embrace it as my life's work. It also gave me the wisdom to understand that whatever I was to have in life, it was up to me to obtain it. While my vision was not always perfect, it sustained me in times of trouble and gave me the courage and strength to find my way through a maze of life's difficulties. I believe that this vision, embedded in my DNA, is something I inherited. I have maximized my genetic potential.

There were, of course, other factors that led me to be able to live the life I led, and luck was clearly one of them. I was lucky to be born to Ludwig and Ilse Boehm and to enjoy a life in the freedom of America. I was lucky to have inherited DNA that allowed me to develop into a good student as well as a healthy and well-balanced individual. One of the luckiest things that happened to me was when I applied to Yale's Surgery Residency program in 1964, and I was interviewed by Dr. James Mark, a plastic surgeon who had not only grown up in Nashville, Tennessee, and attended all the schools I had attended, but his father had been one of our temple's previous rabbis. I still believe to this day that it was the luck of having him as my interviewer that day in New Haven, Connecticut, that helped me gain a spot in the Yale residency program.

That acceptance allowed me to be trained in the place that is considered the birthplace of modern obstetrics, with the introduction of many of the diagnostic and treatment modalities such as electronic fetal monitoring, ultrasonography, treatment of the fetus in utero, and genetic studies, which are now universally utilized. Having been trained at such a unique institution resulted in being asked by Vanderbilt University Medical Center to join the faculty and begin a high-risk obstetrics program. That was luck, and it played a huge role in the success of my entire career.

I felt that, based on my objective and generic definition of a successful life, I was successful, but I still needed to incorporate subjective definitions into my overall definition of a successful life. It was not enough to solely base my success on my genetic background or my environmental influences, nor could I base it totally on elements of luck. Of the numerous definitions of what makes a successful life, the one that seemed to be the most important to me was that a successful life is one that involves loving and being loved.

Many love stories have been told throughout the ages and in many ways mine is not very different. This love story comes from a heart that yearned for a deep, passionate, tender, and committed love and finally found it after many years of disil-lusion and disappointment. What happens during childhood is frequently mentioned as a reason for how we behave later in life. Criminals cite an abusive childhood that led them to a life of crime. Alcoholics claim they grew up in a house filled with addictive behavior, and those who cannot maintain close, loving relationships often state that they were the product of unhappy and unloving parents. I know my early childhood profoundly influenced my life.

I was born to parents who constantly demonstrated their never-ending love for each other, and I wanted that same kind of long and loving relationship in my life. I never considered that I would have anything less. My parents formed a loving bond that helped sustain them for fifty-two years. Surviving poverty during the early years after arriving to America, my parents managed to build a home, raise a son, make close friends, and create a full and rich life. They were committed to each other, doing almost everything together. They never raised their voices and, as far as I could tell, seldom argued. They were clearly in love, and it was fun to watch them and share their joy.

When I met the woman who was to become my first wife, I was a medical student and she a young model. We quickly fell in love and married. It was my plan to spend the rest of my life with my new bride. We had two sons and many wonderful times together; however, somehow it all fell apart. The woman I gave my heart and soul to pulled away. It was the late sixties, and the women's movement, ever so gently at first and more force-fully later, tugged at her heart. I felt her slipping away, but there seemed to be little I could do to maintain our marriage.

There was a short second marriage. As I reflect on this seven-year relationship and try to understand why I chose to remarry soon after my divorce, it became clear that I was weak and hurt from having someone I loved leave me. I needed some-one to help heal my broken heart and also help raise my two sons. Our troubled relationship was filled with significant dif-ferences in our needs and expectations; however, there was one very positive element to our union that I am thankful for every day of my life: the birth of my daughter, Catherine. Catherine was born three years into our marriage, and for a short period of time, she became an anchor to a marriage that should have ended much earlier.

I wasn't looking to get into another relationship, but I was still searching for the love I had seen my parents share. It was at a friend's home on New Year's Day in 1985 that I first met Julie, the woman I would marry and who would become the love of my life, fulfilling all my needs and desires. She was sweet and charming and took my breath away. Friendship blossomed at first, and love followed, a love that consumed my days and nights and brought me to a place where, once again, I could feel the pride of self and the joy of togetherness. It has now been over thirty-five years since that day we met, and our love grows each day. Perhaps what has worked in our marriage is our desire and commitment to bring joy and happiness to each other, as well as being open and honest with our feelings. I was lucky. I had finally found the love I had witnessed as a child in my parents' home, and that love has sustained and nurtured me. It is a love pure and simple and one that has allowed me to feel that my life has been a successful one.

The love I was finally able to attain in my life was augmented by the love that I feel for my children. The moment I held each of my three children in my arms after their births, I was in love. This love did not take time to develop, as most love affairs do. It was instant and intense. Therefore, one of my definitions of a successful life involves the love affair I have had with my three children and why I also asked each of them as well as their spouses to tell me their definitions of a successful life.

My oldest, Todd, is a Vanderbilt graduate and obtained a master's degree in business administration at Tulane University. Currently, he is a computer consultant and project manager for a large computer company. He is married to Jennifer, and together they have two children. He was fifty-one when I posed the question of a successful life to him, and his response was not surprising, since he is the most likely of my children to reduce questions such as this one to its most primary and basic response. "A successful life is when you are satisfied with what you have done." His wife, Jennifer, age forty-six, more loquacious and a school psychologist, added this: "A successful life is one in which you are connected to your family, friends, and community in a meaningful way and one in which you feel as if you have made a contribution in a significant way as well." Todd is happily married, a wonderful provider for his family, involved with his Jewish community, and has very close friends. He is successful in so many ways in his life.

My second child, Thomas, fifty years old, graduated from Vanderbilt University and then obtained a master's degree in counseling psychology and one in divinity. He then obtained a PhD degree from Vanderbilt in special education. Thomas is a professor of special education at Wheaton College, and his wife, Lisa, age forty-two, initially homeschooled their five children. Both wanted to respond to my question together and offered this as their answer to my question of what constituted a successful life. Their response is consistent with their committed involvement with their religion and religious community. "We are born with inherent traits, gifts, personality, and purpose. All these are reflections of God. Some would say we are bestowed with a fragment of the image of God in us. Only we get to reveal to the world this unique facet of God. If we allow these to shine through in our lives, if we give more than we receive, love more than we are loved, and walk with integrity, then we will be successful. When we live out our God-given calling that only we can embody and give our creator the glory, then we are successful." Thomas is an academician, teacher, community leader, husband, father, brother, son, and friend. He is committed to living an ethical and moral life and believes that he is leading a successful life guided by his faith in God.

My youngest child, Catherine, who is also happily married, is thirty-eight years old and a labor and delivery nurse at Northwestern University Hospital in Chicago. She graduated from the University of Georgia and then from Loyola Nursing School in Chicago. Catherine told me that her definition of a successful life is being able to raise her two daughters to be successful. "Success for them will be that they are able to provide for themselves and find happiness and love in their lives. If they are good people, then I will feel successful. My whole purpose in life is to make sure that the next generation is productive, healthy in mind, body, and spirit, and doing good things for their community. Being in a happy and respectful partnership with my husband and being a competent nurse will also help make that goal become a reality. So far I feel successful." Catherine is totally committed to being a good wife and mother. She is a wonderful daughter who is filled with compassion and love, has a warm, embracing manner, and is always thinking of what she can do for others.

Catherine's husband, Eric Kalman, age forty, gave me his definition of a successful life. Ever since Eric came into my life over twelve years ago, I have witnessed warmth, sincerity, and commitment to his family and dedication to an entrepreneurial way of life. "At an early age, I began to create a financial benchmark to ideally exceed when reaching adulthood. Although this initial definition of success in my youth was primarily based around financial position, it allowed me to further explore the financial spectrum within society. I became increasingly aware and concerned over the misfortunes of others and remember many moments and opportunities to donate money for the less fortunate. While the motivation to reach a particular level of financial comfort became a dominant factor as I grew up, I maintained a strong value of a balanced life.

"I have always been aware of the importance of living a healthy life to help prolong the inevitable. This healthy life included regular exercise and eating a healthy diet, and I have extended that lifestyle for myself as well as for my wife and two children. I have concluded that there were four major pillars in my life, including health, friends and family, community, and finances, and these pillars have helped me more clearly understand why this question of what defines a successful life does not always result in a singular response. My fortunes certainly turned when meeting my wife, as we both cared for each other's well-being, and both of us had a strong love for our families and friends and felt a connection with our community responsibilities. My wife shared my major pillars of life!

"Looking back at some of the most important milestones in my life, I realize now the importance of continually evaluating my definition of what constitutes a successful life. I know as I continue to age that spending time with loved ones, helping others, and caring for my family are my committed priorities. Working hard at a profession to provide financial stability and living an honest life with love for family and friends makes me feel successful, and I strive for consistent growth in all aspects with the hope my children will learn and follow in a similar path with strong values to guide them to constantly aim for their successful, yet moving, target."

Listening to the responses of Todd, Thomas, and Catherine and their spouses made me proud of my children and the partners they had chosen to spend their lives with. Success by proxy was reinforced for me as an important component of my definition of a successful life.

The responses from my three children, however, did not tell a complete story. During my years as a resident physician at Yale New Haven Hospital in New Haven, Connecticut, I became a sperm donor for the hospital's fertility clinic. On several occasions during the late 1960s, I provided sperm for women who were unable to conceive, a process which at the time was completely confidential. Little did I realize at the time that almost fifty years later I would meet two of the individuals resulting from my donations.

Neither Karl nor Kama knew they were a product of artificial insemination and only learned of this when they independently sent their DNA to biotechnology company 23andMe for fun. Learning he not only wasn't his father's biological son but that he also had a half-sister, Karl, who lives in Florida, immediately contacted Kama, who lives in New York City. They set up a meeting, marveling at this new development in their lives. Karl then went on a four-month search to find their biological father.

I was surprised but not shocked when I received Karl's letter, followed by Kama's, since the new DNA technology had eliminated any possibility of confidentiality. I understood that this incredible event in my life was an even bigger event in their lives and had more to do with them than with me. I responded to their communication with open arms, and we all agreed to meet, which we did a month later. That weekend meeting in Florida was a very positive experience for all of us, filled with many emotions and the exchange of a large amount of information.

There is no road map for us on how to react or respond to this somewhat unbelievable change in our lives, so we are all taking things one step at a time. My three children reacted very positively when I told them about Karl and Kama and were actually excited to hear they had two additional biological siblings, even making plans to meet one another. Where this is all heading, I do not know. What I do know is that I now have two more children, and I feel it is important to include both Karl's and Kama's definitions of a successful life.

Karl is forty-eight years old, happily married to Isabel, and has two young children. He obtained a master's degree in business, following which he established a wealth management company. Karl answered my question of what he felt determined a successful life. "As a financial advisor, I work with people who look to me to help them reach their financial goals. For many, their financial health is a symbol of their overall success. My clients look to me to guide them. When there is an event that leads to financial stress, they meet with me to express their concern, and they look to me to calm them down when the world around them seems to be collapsing. This has helped me to realize my definition of a successful life. While financial assets give one security and perhaps freedom, they do not define success. I have seen many individuals with every earthly pleasure at their disposal and yet still unfulfilled. When I was in my thirties, I was single and leading a relatively carefree life. At that time, I wanted the comforts that life offered; however, over time I have grown to realize that life is not just about being comfortable and that during our hardest times is when we often grow as human beings. This has all helped me realize that my definition of a successful life is defined by my ability to lead myself, my family, and others close to me on a path to heaven. If my children have everything in this world but have no spiritual connection, I did not succeed. If I have not grown as a man toward what God would want of me, then I also did not succeed."

Kama, fifty years old, has a master's degree from Brandeis University and is a writer for *Sesame Street* and the author of numerous children's books. She wrote me the following: "There are plenty of commonly agreed-upon symbols or measures of a successful life: how many loving friends and family you have, countries you have visited, degrees you have earned, money you have made, people you have helped, books you have published, properties you own, and so on. But to me the real definition of a successful life is one in which you have been able to consider your intentions and then act on them with a full heart. As evidence that I have done this well is that I have many close relationships, but even when some of these relationships have ended, I still consider them successful because of my intent.

"A successful life is one that is largely driven by intentions, no matter what that intention is, and applies even if you never achieve your originally set goal. I intend to prioritize love and being loved, to be of service to those less fortunate, and to pay it forward. I intend to use my creative gifts to help repair the world, to fix, even in a small way, the problems of the world such as threats to wildlife, the class-based inequality in children's literacy levels, or a lack of empathy in our larger culture. I plan to dig deep, make it count, show up, and live big. I intend to fill myself with gratitude and appreciation and not take any of my blessings for granted. I intend to bring the best parts of myself to bear on any challenges I encounter."

Kama continued, "A successful life means discovering the many layers of my heart and then using them for good: my own, my friends', my family's, my colleagues', my community's, and ultimately the world's, and, of course, I will fail plenty. I will fall prey to ego, hesitance, anxiety, laziness, indulgence, or any other human foible. These things will chip away at my chances of success, but eventually, I can always work to bring myself back to the true intention of my heart. In the end, if my actions have been driven by the intentions I have set, I will have had a successful life."

Karl and Kama are wonderful human beings. They are productive and happy in their work. They are loving family members and are active in helping make this world a better place to live. While I can take no nurturing credit for their outcome so far in their lives, I can take some nature credit. What my ancestors passed on to my father and mother was passed on to me, and I in turn passed this same DNA to Todd, Tommy, and Catherine, as well as to Karl and Kama. Their successes have resulted in my feeling a sense of pride for their accomplishments in life, believing that the DNA given to me and passed on to them played a role.

There is one more subjective component to my definition of a successful life. It is to make a positive difference in the lives of others. As a physician and teacher for over fifty years, I believe I am now able to state that this part of my definition has also been achieved. Having delivered approximately ten thousand babies and taught thousands of medical students and hundreds of residents, fellows, and nurses the art and science of medicine, and published several hundred scientific papers, I believe I have made a positive difference in the lives of others. I have also been a member of many nonprofit organizations helping the needy, especially the homeless, through my participation on the board of the Nashville Metro Social Services. I have worked to serve my fellow Jews by serving in a variety of ways on our Jewish Federation Board in Nashville as well as with other Jewish agencies. I have given much of my time and resources to help in repairing the world. I believe I am leaving this world a better place than when I entered it.

So, there it is. My definition of a successful life viewed in an objective manner has been achieved. I was able to maximize my genetic potential and my environmental influence. I have also been able to fulfill the subjective definitions of a successful life. I have loved and been loved by my wife and children, as well as family and a few very close friends. I have also been successful by proxy. Finally, I feel I have made this world a better place. Putting all this together, I believe I can honestly now say that my life has been a successful, as well as a meaningful, one. The question I asked myself several years ago, and which resulted in embarking on the writing of this book, has now been satisfactorily answered.

CHAPTER 7

CONCLUSION

"Success is the ability to go from failure to failure without the loss of enthusiasm." Winston Churchill

"Very little is needed to make a happy life; it is all within yourself, in your way of thinking." Marcus Aurelius

"The unexamined life is not worth living." Socrates

"Life is a journey and death a destination." Jewish prayer

"Intimate loving and enduring relationships with our family and close friends will be among the sources of the deepest joy in our lives." Clayton Christensen

"To laugh often and love much; to win the respect of intelligent persons and the affection of children; to earn the approbation of honest citizens and endure the betrayal of false friends; to appreciate beauty; to find the best in others; to give of one's self; to leave the world a bit better, whether by a healthy

child, a garden patch, or a redeemed social condition; to have played and laughed with enthusiasm and sung with exultation; to know even one life has breathed easier because you have lived . . . this is to have succeeded." Ralph Waldo Emerson

"If I had my life to live all over again, I would have done things a little different. I would have had more friends." Ty Cobb

JUST AS THERE ARE ENDLESS DIFFERENCES IN EACH

individual gene pool that identifies each of us, there are a very large number of definitions of a successful life that also help identify us. One definition does not fit all. After obtaining many definitions of a successful life from a wide spectrum of individuals and professions, from the poor to the wealthy, young to old, I have come to several conclusions.

First and foremost is that Webster's definition does not embrace what most believe to be the real definition of a successful life. Of the more than two hundred individuals I interviewed for this project, very few mentioned having achieved popularity, profit, or distinction as important aspects to the definition of what constituted a successful life. A certain amount of money was necessary to be able to pay for the necessities and a few extras of life; however, even the quite wealthy never mentioned achieving financial wealth as one of their definitions, and fame was not mentioned at all. Even those with considerable fame in their lives did not recognize this status as an important part of their definition of a successful life. Neither Tanya Tucker nor Crystal Gayle believed their fame played a role in their definition of a successful life but, rather, that it had helped in achieving their goal of making the world a better place for them, their children, and countless others.

When people mentioned money, vast sums were never the goal. For example, I was told, "A successful life is having a loving family and a strong faith in God, having a job you enjoy, and being able to go home each day knowing that you are able to pay the bills and have a little savings, and overall being able to enjoy life." Another person mentioned money in a similar fashion. "Being happy with what I have and having enough money to occasionally be able to spend time by the ocean and appreciating the small pleasures that life offers would best define my criteria of a successful life." And someone else said, "Finding love and having enough money to live whatever dream you may have are the basic components of living a successful life." That was about as far as anyone went in exclaiming the virtues of money, although perhaps that is, in part, because most of the definitions given to me were individuals who had sufficient money and were, therefore, able to minimize this aspect of the definition.

One of my interviews, however, made it clear that wealth and money do not contribute to a successful life in the minds of most individuals. When I asked prominent businesswoman Shirley Zeitlin how money affected her definition, she remarked, "Money frees you to not have the stress of the lack of it. It frees you up to do for others, but it does not make you a better or more successful person."

Those in extreme poverty told me that success for them was simply being able to pay for the necessities of life, and while those struggling to merely survive did mention dreams and goals once their ability to survive became a reality, there were no other contemporary definitions for these individuals except that of survival. Some of these dreams and goals included a job that would pay for their lifestyle, raising healthy and well-adjusted children, selling more paintings to the public, being able to deal positively with the pains of life, and being able to help others in need. A reverend I spoke with summed it up best: "Success in life should not be solely defined by socioeconomic status, wealth, and career advancement. Factors such as marriage, family, faith, friendship, character, service, and integrity all matter in living a successful and meaningful life."

Second, I was struck by the number of individuals who said their definitions evolved as they aged. A twenty-eight-year-old told me that success at age fifteen was being able to purchase the coolest tennis shoes, followed by finishing college and graduate school, and then being able to care for his new wife and young daughter. As he matured, his definition evolved again to wanting to be able to attain a lifestyle that allowed for a stress-free life for his family. I asked what his definition would be once this goal was reached. He told me that making the world a better place would probably be his last definition of a successful life.

Former United States congressman from Tennessee Jim Cooper also echoed this opinion regarding a change in definitions as we age. "A successful life's definition is dependent on your age. When I was young, I was very career-oriented, but now my definition has expanded to wanting to leave this world a better place than when I entered it and would now include being a good father, grandfather, and a mentor to many."

Third is the finding that so many of us define success in our lives based on the many experiences we have had in life. One such interview was emblematic of this because Rose was homeless for six months in her early twenties. To her, a successful life involved being able to pay for the necessities of life even though she now lived a life of considerable financial comfort. The same can be said when tragedy strikes family and heart, such as the death of a child. Brenda Rosenblum told me, "When you lose a child, you lose a part of yourself, so it is difficult for me to give you a definition of a successful life since a significant part of me is no longer here. However, the part of me that remains alive believes that my wonderful and loving relationship with my husband, children, grandchildren, and sisters are my crowning definition of a successful life."

Fourth is the fact that most of those who responded listed not one but several definitions, and even then, there was not one specific set of definitions that was universally embraced as the embodiment of a successful life. While there was considerable overlap in definitions of the various age groups, there was a difference in definitions of the young and older individuals. Those in their teens and early twenties equally listed being happy, making a difference in the lives of others, and having a good job and career as their three top definitions, while individuals over the age of seventy-five equally listed making a positive impact in life and having a loving family and good friends as their top three.

Following their top three definitions, the young listed, in order of frequency, the importance of financial security, having good friends and a loving family, handling adversity, following your dreams, having a plan in life, being educated, being content with the life you have, having few regrets, living a moral and ethical life, living a life of faith, being grateful, and living a life of which you were proud.

The maturing age group listed as their number-one definition making the world a better place, with enjoying one's work and career being a close second. These two definitions were followed by having good friends and a loving family, having goals and dreams, being happy, having financial security, being grateful, living a moral and ethical life, not being afraid to die, having a healthy body, living a life with lifelong learning, being kind and respectful, never giving in to adversity, being in the right mind, having a strong faith, having well-adjusted and happy children, having no major regrets, learning from your mistakes, and living a life of which your mother would be proud.

The mature age group most frequently mentioned having a positive effect on the lives of others, closely followed by having good friends and a loving family, having a strong religious faith, and having a career and job you truly enjoyed. These definitions were followed in smaller numbers by success by proxy, being grateful, having few regrets, being kind and respectful to others, achieving financial security, living a purposeful life, living a life of continuous education, having a good reputation, having taken care of one's body and mind, living a life of forgiveness and compassion, having mental calmness, loving life, living a moral and ethical life, having wonderful memories, having a good sense of humor, being creative and artistic, being happy, overcoming fear, beating back family demons, living by the Boy Scout creed, doing it "my way," being in the moment, being able to take care of oneself, having reasonable expectations, and having peace in one's life.

The older age group of individuals over seventy-five years of age equally listed making a positive impact in the lives of others and having a loving family and good friends as their leading definitions of a successful life. These were followed by loving and being loved, following one's dreams, being a good person, living by the Golden Rule, success by proxy, being able to deal with adversity, using God's gifts of talent and abilities to benefit others, minimizing the negative influences of mistakes, being happy, having blessed memories, living by the Boy Scout creed, having a job or career you enjoy, putting a smile on someone's face, being content with what you have, and avoiding stress.

Fifth is the fact that the definition of making a positive difference in the lives of others and leaving the world a better place was the most popular definition of a successful life in each of the four age categories. Regardless of age, that this was the most common definition would indicate that despite one's age, most individuals define a successful life with the desire to make the world a better place. While there were many other definitions, this definition was the most mentioned. Despite his fame and fortune, from a young age, all former senator Bob Corker wanted to do with his life was to leave the world a better place for others. We all want to feel as if our lives had some type of purpose and meaning and that we will be remembered as someone who contributed in some manner to the well-being of the world we lived in. That well-being included sharing love and support of family, healing the sick, comforting the depressed, helping the homeless, feeding the hungry, clothing the naked, and a host of other noble activities that exemplified sharing of one's resources, time, and effort. This definition of wanting to make a positive impact on the lives of others or on the world overall seems to be a universal definition and is mentioned in some fashion or another by many of those interviewed in each of the age groups. I believe this to be a comforting finding as it also turns out that making the world a better place is a critical element in society's survival.

Jonathan Sacks, a rabbi and theologian, wrote in his discussion of one of Deuteronomy's passages that "suffering, persecution, a common enemy, unite a people and turn it into a nation. But freedom, affluence, and security turn a nation into a collection of individuals each pursuing his or her own happiness, often indifferent to the fate of those who have less, the lonely, the marginal, and the excluded. When that happens, societies start to disintegrate. At the height of their good fortune, the long slow process of decline begins. The only way to avoid it, said the biblical Moses, is to share your happiness with others and, in the midst of that collective, national celebration, serve God. Blessings are not measured by how much we own or earn or spend or possess but by how much we share."[18]

Erik Erikson's stages of psychosocial development are a comprehensive psychoanalytical theory that identifies a series of eight stages that a healthy developing individual should pass through from infancy to late adulthood.[19] It is his eighth stage that speaks to us of a successful life, as it describes wisdom as the virtue of those sixty years of age and older and is a time when an individual reflects on his or her life. "As we grow older and become senior citizens, we tend to slow down our productivity and explore life as a retired person. It is during this time that we contemplate our accomplishments and are able to develop integrity if we see ourselves as leading a successful life. If we see our life as unproductive or feel that we did not accomplish our life goals, we become dissatisfied with life and develop despair, often leading to depression and hopelessness. The final development task is retrospective: people look back on their lives and accomplishments. They develop feelings of contentment and integrity if they believe that they have had a happy, productive life."

Ever since my first year in medical school when I spent a considerable amount of time dissecting a cadaver to study the anatomy of the human body, I concluded that life after death did not involve the physical body. To me it consisted primarily of the memories and deeds that my life created and that I would eventually leave those deeds and memories to my loved ones and friends in an everlasting fashion. It has been said that we actually die twice. First when we take our last breath and then again when the last person who remembers us dies. However, during those early medical school years, it seemed that there needed to be more extension to this belief in life after death and it should not end merely when the last person who remembers us dies.

I eventually came to believe that the words of wisdom I spoke during my lifetime, the good deeds I performed, and the values I lived by would in some fashion be passed not merely to those I loved and knew but that these same individuals would then in turn pass some aspect of my life's wisdom and good deeds to those they knew and loved, from generation to generation in quite vivid memory initially and then later only as an echo of who I was in much more subtle ways that would be difficult to trace or understand.

It seemed that I am who I am much because my father and mother left me with not only genetic traits and characteristics but also a moral and ethical code of behavior, what could be viewed as "spiritual DNA." They in turn received their spiritual DNA from their parents and friends who received theirs in similar fashion. In essence, therefore, I am in so many ways the product of relatives and others who passed down to me physical and spiritual DNA over many generations. This would explain a doctrine of living long after we die or being remembered by anyone alive. In that sense, we can feel as though we are able to leave this world a better place and can have a positive impact on the lives of so many for generations to come.

Writing in his book *21 Lessons for the 21st Century*, Yuval Noah Harari wrote that it is difficult to leave behind something tangible such as our DNA or a poem, but that perhaps it was still possible to make this world a better place. It just depended on how one defined leaving this world a better place. He stated you can help somebody, and that somebody will subsequently help somebody else, and you thereby contribute to the overall improvement of the world and constitute a small link in the great chain of kindness. "Maybe you serve as a mentor to a difficult child who goes on to become a physician and saves the lives of many? There are so many ways in which to make this world a better place. Through works of love, kindness, thoughtfulness, generosity, supporting and comforting others, healing the mind and body of others, raising and nurturing healthy children, teaching a future generation and advancing science are just a few of the ways in which each of us can make this world a better place."[20]

Fortunately, many individuals in history had an earnest desire to make a difference, wanting to be remembered for leaving our world a better place. As an example, one of our greatest presidents, George Washington, chaired the convention that ultimately led to the adoption of the United States Constitution. Although Washington at first hesitated, James Madison successfully argued that if Washington did not accept this vital role, "the republic would fail, and Washington's legacy would be forgotten. Washington wanted to be remembered, like the heroes of classical antiquity that he'd been taught to admire since boyhood, as the founder of a great republic. That was his private ambition."[21] And in his most recent book on gene editing, *Code Breaker,* Walter Isaacson opined that "all of the scientists I write about in this book say that their main motivation is not money, or even glory, but the chance to unlock the mysteries of nature and use those discoveries to make the world a better place."[22]

My sixth conclusion was that a considerable number of interviewees mentioned the importance of having good friends during life as one of the most important definitions of a successful life. Sometime around 350 BC the Greek philosopher Aristotle listed three types of friendships, which I believe remain applicable today.[23] The first he labeled as the "friendship of utility," which was the kind of friend you find convenient to have in your life. These are the people you work and play with without coming to know each other deeply. The second type of friendship he calls the "friendship of pleasure," and this is the friend in your life whom you spend more time with at lunches, dinners, sporting events, and social outings, to name a few. This type of friend is one with whom you may spend casual time, but the relationship never tips over into something more serious.

The last type, which Aristotle calls the "friendship of the good," is one that is quite rare in life. This type of friendship is one in which you become soul mates, understanding each other at a fundamental core, and this is the friend with whom you express some of your innermost thoughts and feelings. There is just about nothing that you would not discuss with the friend of the good. There is true respect, trust, and acceptance of this type of friend, with an element of love entwined. We are lucky if we have just a few of these types of friends. While friends of pleasure are important and critical to a life of friendships, I believe that when friendships were mentioned in the definition of a successful life, it was the friendship of the good that most people were describing. To have just a few of these friends of the good would suffice in most people's minds as part of their definition of a successful life.

Seventh is that even the youngest individuals often had definitions that went beyond the more typical definition of happiness and career. Some of these definitions included: having used whatever gift God has given you in the most productive manner; not backing down in the face of adversity; following your dreams and using what you are good at; having the motivation and courage to keep trying and never give up; having a plan for your life and being prepared for the hard times that await you; having the drive and focus in pursuing goals; responding to obstacles with motivation and perseverance rather than with despondence; having enough money to sustain a comfortable lifestyle; having a family that you love; making a contribution to society, both politically as well as philanthropically; having few regrets and having lived an honest, embracing, ethical, and moral life; and leaving behind a legacy, so as not to be forgotten.

While these young individuals were for the most part optimistic about their future, there are some in our society who worry about our young people being able to fulfill their dreams to create a happy and meaningful life. Yale professor William Deresiewicz is one of these individuals. In his book *Excellent Sheep: The Miseducation of the American Elite and the Way to a Meaningful Life*, Deresiewicz states that our elite universities are failing to equip college students with the skills necessary for finding happiness and pursuing a meaningful life. "We have constructed an educational system that produces highly intelligent, accomplished 22-year-olds who have no idea what they want to do with their lives: no sense of purpose and, what is worse, no understanding of how to go about finding one."[24] If Deresiewicz is right, we will need to rethink how we educate our young people in America, so as to give them a realistic foundation for achieving a meaningful and successful life.

Eighth is that while there clearly are common themes in defining a successful life, I was surprised at many of the outlier definitions. Some of these include: not being afraid to die, living a life of faith in God, having few regrets, being successful by proxy, living by the Boy Scout's creed, being grateful about the small and large things in life, being able to accept yourself and no longer looking for validation from other people, having wonderful memories, being able to laugh at yourself and at life around you, having an absence of conflict with family and friends, being able to beat back family demons, taking on jobs that no one else wanted to do, having taken good care of the wonderful body and mind given to you, having a long and happy marriage, putting a smile on someone's face, being open to change, being able to pursue one's dreams, and being able to fall asleep easily without the hypothetical future on one's mind.

That there are many outlier definitions was made perfectly clear to me when I interviewed Dan, who was homeless, and who told me that he already felt that his life was successful as he felt his life was successful each time he sold one of his acrylic paintings on the streets of Nashville. "Money is a tool," he told me, "just like the acrylic for my paintings. It does not define success for me." And Lee Stewart told me, "At age seventy, I have finally learned that a successful life involves equanimity in trying to maintain mental calmness, composure, and evenness of temper, especially when I feel under pressure with a difficult situation or person or dealing with a deadline."

Another outlier definition came from someone who told me that a successful life to her was being in her right mind. She explained that when she was nineteen years old, she had served in the military and was a part of Operation Desert Storm, where she had witnessed many of her fellow soldiers develop post-traumatic stress disorder and that this affliction had caused them to live a life of sadness and illness. These colleagues were not in their right mind, and so it was her belief that if she could maintain a life of being in her right mind, she would be successful.

There were several other outlier definitions. "Being successful includes creating and then enjoying experiences that allow for many wonderful memories, which then allows for good feelings and contentment." Another suggested, "Just looking back on your life and being able to say that you did it your way. A successful life is a life of forgiveness and honor. I feel the most successful when I honor my love ones; forgiving them is my path to success."

Ninth is that so many respondents included the word *love* in their definitions. Having a loving family, being loved, and having someone to love were the most common phrases used. Love is truly a universal feeling that has been beautifully described in prose, poetry, song, feelings, and actions since the recording of time. Love is the selfless expression that manifests itself in the recognition of another's ego. It is the tireless energy of existence and the tenderness of self. Love takes time to fertilize and grow. It demands a feeling of caring and respect. It has the power to bring joy to the heart and comfort to the soul. Only with the birth of a child do we possess the ability to experience the instantaneous feeling of love. All other loving relationships take time and nurturing, but when love appears in our lives, it is one of our greatest gifts, which leads to a successful life.

It is not surprising, therefore, that when asked for a definition of a successful life, so many individuals placed love at or near the top of their lists. To be loved and to love brings peace and contentment to the soul and allows for a feeling of achieving success. Two of the respondents in the older group and who had been married for a very long time made no attempt to offer a list of definitions. Theirs was a singular one that speaks of love: "The key to a successful life is a long and happy marriage," and

"A successful life is about marrying the right partner, one who has a good sense of humor and self-esteem, is thoughtful, kind, fair, and wise and believes in you, represents and advises you, and is a model for your children; one who is also able to help solve those challenges that are inevitable in a lifetime." For these two individuals, there was nothing more important to mention than loving and being loved.

Pat Rose, sixty-seven years old, happily married, and a long-time friend, told me that "a successful life is having people who love me. If I have earned people's love, that would mean I have done something right, and it would also mean that I have people to love. Love is what makes life successful." Harvard professor Clayton Christensen also said it well in his book *How Will You Measure Your Life?* "Intimate, loving, and enduring relationships with our family and close friends will be among the sources of the deepest joy in our lives."[25]

Tenth is the finding that many of the respondents mentioned their faith in God in their definition of a successful life. "A successful life is one where I can teach my daughter about God's strength and his wondrous works so that she can pass them to the next generation." "Experiencing joy by first knowing the talents you have, then exercising those talents to benefit others, and most importantly, giving God the glory." "To live a life in God's favor by using his many blessings to treat others fairly, raise a healthy, strong family, be respected in the community, and offer help to those less fortunate." One person told me that each morning he recites a prayer to remind him to love God and that a successful life to him was being able to live out the words of the morning prayer that commands him to practice lovingkindness for himself and others.

Faith plays a large role for many in their determination of whether their life is successful. "We are born with inherent traits, gifts, personality, and purpose. All these are reflections of God. Some would say we are bestowed with a fragment of the image of God in us. Only we get to reveal to the world this unique facet of God. If we allow these to shine through in our lives, if we give more than we receive, love more than we are loved, and walk with integrity, then we will be successful." Another person told me that a successful life for him was one in which he followed a life in Christ. "That way of life gives me the best chance of living an almost perfect life."

Eleventh on my list of conclusions is that, while I opined it difficult to categorize those who shared their definitions into various socioeconomic classes, it was also difficult to find significant differences in the various age groups I chose. The differences based on age groups was noted in young individuals interviewed compared to the older group. Those in the fourteen to twenty-four age group listed being happy, making the world a better place, and loving what you do career-wise as the top three most often mentioned definitions of a successful life, while those in the over seventy-five years old group listed as their three most mentioned definitions having a loving family and friends, making a positive difference in the lives of others, and fulfilling dreams and goals. The maturing age group's top definitions were making the world a better place, followed equally by enjoying the work you do and having a loving family, while the mature group's top definitions were making a positive impact on the lives of others, having a loving family and friends, having faith in God, and finding a career or job you enjoy.

Finally, while I thought those individuals in poverty or with disabilities would not easily fit in the age categories I established for this book, I found that even the very poor had dreams and goals beyond their current survival mode, and those with intellectual challenges had definitions that were consistent with the degree of their disability. Some of the poor had much to say about their definitions of a successful life. "A successful life is one in which you deal with the real pains of life and are able to come out the other side in a positive way and that you have taken something of value from those experiences." "A successful life to me is to never give up and being a strong woman and a good example for my kid." "If my son, who is now seven years old, can be raised in a happy environment, and when he is an adult that he will be able to take care of himself, then I will feel successful." "A successful life is one in which I am financially stable. I want a career, not just a job. I want to start a cleaning business to help achieve these things."

The individuals with intellectual disabilities I interviewed, regardless of age, also echoed the fact that their condition did not rob them of a clear and ongoing definition of a successful life. "A successful life is enjoying what I have, which are the good memories of the moments I have with my family and friends." "A successful life for me is getting a job and being able to take care of myself and living alone." "Success to me is to be able to comb my hair, brush my teeth, shave, and be able to take care of myself as well as to take care of my room."

We define and measure so much in our lives today that it would seem important to also attempt to define what a successful life for us would look like. While most of those responding to the question did so with subjective definitions, the objective definition also worked for some, especially when individuals began to use it as a template for their definition. Regardless, defining our successful life and then periodically measuring how we are doing in achieving that definition would seem to be a valuable process for all of us to undertake. It can merely be whether we have been able to maximize our genetic potential and environmental influences or that we have been able to overcome negative genetic potential and environmental influences, as was the case of Kerry Brock, who overcame her demons while growing up, and Jeff Sonsino, who also overcame certain nature and nurture influences, as well as Billy Hudson, who clearly was able to minimize his torturous environment as a child. This objective measure of a successful life should, however, be augmented by subjective definitions as well. Both are valuable methods of defining a successful life and allow for a very large proportion of individuals of all ages and statuses in life to be able to ascertain whether their lives have indeed been successful.

Many stated that a part of the definition of a successful life was being able to accept yourself for who you are. It is important to reach a point in life where you forgive yourself for mistakes made or for not being able to achieve many of the goals that were planned in life. We all make mistakes in life, and these mistakes are signs of being actively involved in life's many adventures. To take risks and fail is part of each of our lives, and we must learn to forgive ourselves and move on. These mistakes in actions or judgment often make us better human beings.

The same can be said about the definition of setting goals in life. Without something to aim for, we lose so much of the excitement that life has to offer, even when we reach old age. I am retired and eighty years old, yet I am still setting goals for my life. Without these ambitions and goals, we reduce our ability to live a successful life.

By periodically rethinking whether your life is successful, you can set goals and objectives in an attempt to fulfill that definition. Defining a successful life should be something we all undertake throughout our lives. And as Dr. Wright Pinson clearly stated, "This question of a successful life is one that is usually attempted to be answered and expanded upon at some- one's funeral. We should attempt to answer that question for our- selves before our funeral."

To periodically define what our elements of a successful life are and to ascertain if we are living up to that definition, we must overcome the problem of unawareness. I marvel at the ability of humans to properly function while being totally unaware of their surroundings. I am referring specifically to that car ride home when suddenly you arrive and realize you do not remember the actual drive or any familiar landmarks you passed. Even though your mind was obviously deep in thought and somewhere else, you were still able to send appropriate signals to arms, legs, and eyes to allow safe passage through heavy traffic, changing lights, and stop signs.

A state of happiness can also result from an individual being consistently aware of his or her surroundings and being able to experience the moment with a rich feeling of being alive and present. Such was the case with Howard Korn, who told me that being and living in the moment, along with being grateful and aware of life's evolving events, have been major contributors to his ability to enjoy his life and consider it successful even as he continued to fight a lengthy battle with cancer.

Many years ago, I encountered a patient who taught me an important lesson on this subject of awareness being a critical ingredient of happiness. I was in Southern California studying cancer at the City of Hope. I was twenty-nine years old, finishing my obstetrics-gynecology training, and now taking time out to concentrate and focus on the art and science of cancer surgery. My responsibilities included working in the breast cancer clinic. There I would see approximately twenty patients every Wednesday afternoon, most of whom had advanced cancer of the breast and were returning weekly to receive their chemotherapy treatments.

It was in the middle of one of these clinics, while going from room to room, that I walked into one and sat down to speak with a middle-aged woman I had seen before who had advanced metastatic breast cancer. The tumor had spread to her lungs, making it difficult for her to speak. Words came slowly and with great effort, and while we had spoken before on other visits, our times together had been perfunctory and businesslike. As we sat together in that small examining room, I sat back in my chair and, speaking softly, inquired as to how she was doing. Her response still echoes in my mind today as she uttered with a smile, "Wonderful." Somewhat taken aback, I remarked how interesting it was that such cheerfulness filled her at a time of such obvious illness. She replied, "The best thing that ever happened to me, doctor, was the day I was told I had cancer."

"How could that be?" I asked.

"Well, doctor, before I knew I had cancer, I never really saw the sun rise or set, and I was never aware of all the wonderful things life had to offer. I went through each day on auto-drive much like the times I drove home from work but was unaware of the drive until the moment I pulled into my garage. But since that day, knowing each day was limited and therefore precious, I began to notice the sunset and the sunrise. I heard sounds I never heard before. I smelled fragrances, tasted food, and touched textures as never before. All at once I became alive and richness filled my every day."

With eyes slightly moist, I finished my exam and treatment, and as I turned to leave, she responded, "Just think of it, doctor. You could start all that today, without cancer." Three weeks later she took her last breath and died quietly in her hospital bed. When I pulled the sheet over her placid face, I knew that a great lesson had been given to me that I would not forget.

Unfortunately, many of us too often go through life with much the same experience. We work and play yet are not truly aware of our surroundings or any real aspect of the experience itself. We do not savor the moment and, therefore, cannot bring awareness to an appropriate level. In other words, we often go through life much like that car ride, suddenly finding that life is over and we had not really been aware to truly enjoy the moment. It is, however, not easy to train oneself to become aware. It is a feat that must be practiced before it can become a daily part of life's routine.

Too many of us have difficulties living in the present. We glorify the past and look to the future to give us pleasure or peace. In fact, the good old days are now, not then nor necessarily in the future. I believe we can and should become more aware of each moment of our lives. We must awaken from our sleepwalking by sharpening our senses so that we can view the beauty of nature that surrounds us, taste the food we eat, smell the wonderful fragrance of flowers, and feel the wind in our faces and the love that surrounds us. In this way, we will not remain unaware of our drive through life. Walter Isaacson, writing in his book on Leonardo Da Vinci, stated, "I did learn from Da Vinci how a desire to marvel about the world that we encounter each day can make each moment of our lives richer."[26]

As we age, it becomes increasingly clear what our definitions of a successful life are and whether we have or have not led a successful life. The bar for living a successful life need not necessarily be a high one. A world in which there are vast numbers of individuals from young to old, from rich to poor, from laborer to professional, from religious to atheist, from parent to childless, from gifted to average, and from healthy to compromised, is a world that values the total worth and vast differences of all human beings in a most egalitarian manner. When the time comes for our lives to end, we should be able to appropriately evaluate our lives as successful or not. From the over two hundred individual definitions outlined in this book, it is my belief that a vast majority of all of us will be able to view our lives in the rearview mirror and feel that we have indeed lived a life of success.

For a variety of reasons, however, it may not seem possible for some to believe that they can achieve a successful life, because numerous obstacles in their path may impede their ability to feel as if their lives have been worthwhile and meaningful. However, even with interfering obstacles, there are ways for many of us to create a definition that works for the life we have lived. A life of illness can still be a life filled with friends and faith. A life of disability can still be a life filled with gratefulness and pride in what one has been able to accomplish. A life of loss or sorrow can still be a life filled with helping others and making this world a better place. A life of poverty can still be a life filled with pride by raising children who accomplish a life of success on their own. A life of unfulfilling employment can still be a life filled with family, friends, and faith.

In his summation of a successful life, Rabbi Mark Schiftan had this to say: "If you are actively grateful for all you have been blessed with in your life and are able to be thankful for every day, and if you are able to measure yourself by the advancements you have made from the beginning to the end of your life and respond to adversity in a consistently positive manner at each crossroad and challenging chapter, and if you have lived a life filled with love and loving relationships measured in tangible acts and expressions of that love for others and fashioned a life that brings blessings to others, to all those whom you encounter and embrace throughout your life, then I believe you will have lived a successful life."

NOTES

1. Yuval Noah Harari, *21 Lessons for the 21st Century* (New York: Spiegel and Grau, 2019), 187.
2. Evan Thomas, *First: Sandra Day O'Connor* (Random House, 2019), 119.
3. Simon Sinek, *Start with Why: How Great Leaders Inspire Everyone to Take Action* (Portfolio/Penguin, 2011), 179–82.
4. Sinek, *Start with Why.*
5. Gallop Poll, 2016 Robert Bird, Frank Newport. Gallup http://news.gallup.com/opinion/polling-matters/204497/determines-americans-perceive-social-class.aspx
6. Clay Stauffer, "Rethinking happiness, morality and success," *Tennessean*, September 28, 2019, www.tennessean.com
7. Dave Schools, "I took Yale's most popular class ever, and it completely changed how I spend my money," Contributor@daveschools, May 13, 2019.
8. Jonathon Rauch, "Why Prosperity Has Increased but Happiness Has Not," (opinion) *New York Times*, August 21, 2018.
9. Gallop Poll, "Can Money Bring Happiness?" July 2, 2019, University of Illinois
10. David Lykken and Auke Tellegen, "Minnesota Twin Family Study," August 29, 2007.

11. Arthur Brooks, TED Talk, Key to "Achieving Happiness." December 14, 2013, www.youtube.com

12. "Trends in Psychological Well-Being, 1972–2014 General Social Survey," Final Report, NORC at the University of Chicago.

13. Arthur C. Brooks, "Meaningful Work, Not Money, Makes People Happy," *New York Times*, December 14, 2013.

14. Gore Vidal, www.brainyreads.com

15. Hilary Brueck and Samantha Lee, "This is why our phones are making us miserable," *Business Insider*, March 24, 2018.

16. Harold Kushner, *When Bad Things Happen to Good People* (Random House, 1981).

17. Ben Sasse, *Them: Why We Hate Each Other—and How to Heal* (New York: St. Martin's Press), 44.

18. Jonathan Sacks, *Covenant Conversation in Collective Joy* (Re'eh 5779).

19. Erik H. Erikson and Joan M. Erikson, *The Life Cycle Completed, Extended Version* (W.W. Norton, 1998).

20. Harari, *21 Lessons for the 21st Century*, 286.

21. David M. Rubenstein, *The American Story* (New York: Simon and Schuster, 2019), 12.

22. Walter Isaacson, *Code Breaker* (New York: Simon and Schuster, 2021), 475.

23. Book VIII of *Nicomachean Ethics*

24. William Deresiewicz, *Excellent Sheep: The Miseducation of America's Elite* (New York: Free Press, 2014).

25. Clayton Christensen, *How Will You Measure Your Life?* (Harper Collins, 2012).

26. Walter Isaacson, *Leonardo da Vinci*, (New York: Simon and Schuster, 2017) 7.

INDEX

changing definitions of, 49–50,
115, 183
financial achievement and, 10–11
importance of asking ourselves
about the components of a,
154–155, 199
individual definitions of, xi
influence of age on, xiv–xv
interfering obstacles to, 203
objective and generic definition of,
xi–xiii, 138, 159, 166–167, 198
outlier, 192–194
people interviewed for, xiii–xiv
summation of a, 203–204
using tools on hand for, 125–126
Support from family and friends,
39, 59, 79, 83, 85, 107, 114–115,
119, 159
Surveys
about work satisfaction, 42
on impact of income on happiness,
10
Survival, defining a successful life
and, 11, 13, 18–19

T

Tackett, Judy, 55
Talent(s)
impact of the gift of, 5
maximizing your, 134
Talmud, viii
Teenagers, 32–34
TennCare, 70–71
Them (Sasse), 44
Trachtman, Sy, 131
Tragedy, definition of a successful
life changing because of, 184
Tran, Kaylon, 86
Travel, 116
True to one's self, being, 109, 140
Tucker, Risa L., 124
Tucker, Tanya, 67–69

21 Lessons for the 21st Century
(Harari), 3, 189
Twin studies, 41

U

Unconditional giving, 74
Unconditional love, 57, 87, 88, 152,
159
Unhappiness, loneliness and, 44
Upper class, 8, 9, 10
Upper-middle class, 9
Urban areas, social class and, 9

V

Values
doing for others because of your,
102
happiness influenced by our, 41
identifying and supporting your,
38–39
passing down to others, 150, 188
respecting other people's, 121
Vance, J.D., 10
Vanderbilt University Medical
Center, x
Vanderbilt University students, 35–39
Vaughn, Demetria, 59
Venick, Irwin, 117
Vision, genetic gift of, 160–161,
165–166
Volunteering, 16, 17, 109, 121, 152–153

W

Walker, Stanley, 18
Washington, George, 190
Webb, Wandria, 53
Weinstein, Ivan, 22
Westman, Mickey, 150
*When Bad Things Happen to Good
People* (Kushner), 43
Wilson, Teresa, 60
Wilson-Liverman, Angela, 60

*Deceased

ABOUT THE AUTHOR

DR. FRANK H. BOEHM IS PROFESSOR EMERITUS IN the Department of Obstetrics and Gynecology at Vanderbilt University Medical Center. He was on the faculty for forty-seven years, specializing in the field of maternal fetal medicine. Dr. Boehm, a nationally known expert in the field of electronic fetal monitoring, has authored over 250 scientific papers as well as two books that deal with patient-physician relationships, *Doctors Cry, Too* and *Building Patient/Doctor Trust*, which were based on his eighteen-year "Healing Words" bi-monthly op-ed columns in the *Tennessean*. For fifteen years, Boehm served as the chair of the Vanderbilt University Medical Center Ethics Committee and vice chair of the Department of Obstetrics and Gynecology. He has received numerous prestigious teaching awards at Vanderbilt, one of which is in his name. In 2014 Boehm received the coveted Human Relations Award from Community Nashville. Dr. Boehm has been a prominent leader in the Nashville Jewish community, serving as president of the Nashville Jewish Federation and the Nashville Jewish Foundation. Boehm and his wife, Julie, live in Nashville, Tennessee, and Boca Raton, Florida.